F.

£5.00

The Rabbit Fancier; a Treatise Upon the Breeding, Rearing, Feeding, and General Management of Rabbits

THE

RABBIT FANCIER;

A TREATISE UPON THE

Breeding, Rearing, Feeding, and General Management

OF

RABBITS:

WITH REMARKS UPON THEIR

DISEASES AND REMEDIES,

DRAWN FROM AUTHENTIC SOURCES AND PERSONAL OBSERVATION.

TO WHICH ARE ADDED

FULL DIRECTIONS FOR THE CONSTRUCTION OF HUTCHES, RABBITRIES, ETC.,
TOGETHER WITH RECIPES FOR COOKING AND DRESS-
ING FOR THE TABLE.

BY C. N. BEMENT,

AUTHOR OF "THE AMERICAN POULTERER'S COMPANION."

NEW YORK:

C. M. SAXTON & CO., AGRICULTURAL BOOK PUBLISHERS,
152 FULTON STREET.
1855.

Entered, according to Act of Congress, in the year 1855, by

C. M. SAXTON,

in the Clerk's Office of the District Court of the United States, in and for the Southern District of New York.

Edward O. Jenkins, Printer,
NOS. 26 AND 28 FRANKFORT STREET.

ILLUSTRATIONS.

CONTENTS.

PREFATORY.

In the preparation of this little treatise, it has been the aim and desire of the author that without entirely excluding the less necessary points of the subject, it should be made as practicable as possible, and should contain such information as is most required by beginners, with but little previous knowledge of the management of our little favorite. We have done our best to carry out this intention, and we think that the novice, after a careful perusal of the following pages, will find but little difficulty in commencing and continuing his pleasing task.

When about twelve or thirteen years of age we commenced breeding rabbits,—the common tame varieties, black, blue, white, and party-colored. For their accommodation we enclosed a circular piece of ground, on a side-hill, about twenty-five feet in diameter, by setting boards on end in the ground, two feet deep, and about five feet high, in the form of a stockade, or like the enclosure of the pit, as figured in page 39. We dug a pit in the centre, covering it with boards, placing the earth on the top in the form of a mound. From this they worked holes in the sides of the walls and formed their nests for breeding.

We started with a trio, one buck and two does. They

"bred like rabbits," and we soon had quite a stock, say from fifteen to twenty, but for some reason they did not seem to increase much afterward. The cause at the time we could not comprehend, but now think the bucks or males caused the mischief by destroying the young, and quarrelling with one another, so we abandoned that enterprise. Breeding in hutches, at that early date, was unknown in this country.

While residing on Three Hills Farm, some eighteen years ago, my father, being crippled with rheumatism, amused himself with breeding rabbits in hutches, and succeeded admirably; raising quite a large number, many of which afforded us dainty meals. Castrating the young bucks and fattening them for the table, many of them weighed eight pounds after being dressed. The flesh was white, tender, and well-flavored.

We hope that this little book will serve to diffuse, more widely, reliable information on the subject of which it treats, and prove a welcome acquisition and manual of present interest and permanent utility; and that it will claim, at least, the favorable consideration of those for whom it is designed.

C. N. BEMENT.

Staten Island, May, 1855.

RABBITS.

In a little treatise like this, it is hardly worth the labor to inquire into the origin, or to attempt to trace the subjugation of the rabbit. Like the domestic fowl, its domestication is shrouded in mystery. The wild rabbit is undoubtedly the origin of our various domestic breeds. It is generally believed that the rabbit was first introduced into Spain from Africa, by the Romans, whence it gradually spread, naturalizing itself into temperate climates, but does not reach quite so far north as the hare. There appears every probability that the most remarkable varieties came from Persia and the adjacent countries.

Tame races, which have the greatest claim to style themselves aboriginals of England, were in all likelihood existing in their present state long before the commencement of any historical epoch in Great Britain. It would appear, therefore, that the rabbit is not an aboriginal of England, but the date of its introduction is unknown. Tame rabbits easily resume their natural state of freedom, and return to their instinctive habits.

In its wild state, it forms long, winding burrows; keeps its hole by day; feeds morning, evening, and night, on vegetables and grain.

Rabbits are found in great numbers in England, burrowing in dry, sandy soils, particularly if the situation be

1*

hilly or the ground irregular. Enclosures called *warrens*
are frequently made in England, in favorable spots of this
kind, some of which extend to hundreds of acres. Rabbits not being swift-footed animals, are taken by nets,
traps, ferrets, and dogs. The common wild rabbit is of a
gray color, and is the best for the purpose of food; its
skin is valuable, as the pelt is a material for hats; but
another variety has been introduced, the *silver-gray*, the
skin of which is more valuable, and is dressed as fur; the
color of this is a black ground, thickly interspersed with
single gray hairs. A great number of them are exported
to China.

Size excepted, the rabbit closely resembles the hare in
all its principal characters. It may, however, be at once
distinguished by the comparative shortness of the head
and ears, as well as of the hinder limbs; the absence of a
black tip to the ears; and by the brown color of the upper
surface of the tail. Its habits and general economy are
totally opposite to the hare, and its flesh, instead of being
dark and highly flavored, is white and delicate. The
flesh of the rabbit differs somewhat according to its wild
or domestic state. There is some difference of opinion as
to which is preferable; the wild rabbit has more flavor,
but some prefer the tame as whiter and more delicate.

The tame rabbit in all its varieties, has always been, and
still is, a great favorite in many parts of the European
Continent. "In Holland," says a writer in the American
Agriculturist, "it is bred with reference to color only,
which must be a pure white, with dark ears, feet, legs and
tail; this distribution has a singular effect, but withal, it
is a pretty little creature. The French breed a long,

rangy animal, of great *apparent* size, but deficient in depth and breadth, and, of course, wanting in constitution; no attention is paid to color, and its markings is matter of accident. The white Angola, with its beautiful long fur and red eyes, is also a great favorite in France."

Albinos are sometimes found among the common white rabbits, and it often happens that one or two appear in a litter, when neither of the parents are so.

There are several varieties of tame rabbits. The large white and yellow, and white variety, have the whitest and most delicate flesh, and when cooked in the same way, sometimes rivals the turkey. There is also a large variety of the hare color, the flesh of which is highly flavored and more savory than that of the common rabbit; and it makes a good dish cooked like the hare, to which, at six or eight months old, it is nearly equal in size.

As the flesh of the tame rabbit is inclined to be dry, it is well to feed them partly on green vegetables, which makes it more juicy. They become larger and fatter in the tame than in the wild state; but it is not desirable to have them as fat as they can be made. Some that have been fed in hutches have been known to exceed twelve pounds in weight. When very old they are tough like hares.

Wild rabbits are procurable young and in good condition only at particular seasons, but tame ones may be always bred in a state fit for the table. The latter are in the greatest perfection when four months old; but if well fed, will not be too old at eighteen months old.

The skins, if carefully preserved, besides being saleable, are useful in a family for lining garments.

MERITS AND USES.

THE real value of the rabbit to man is greater than would appear at first sight. Independently of the fur, which enters largely into the manufacture of hats and other articles, the skin makes an excellent glue. If the flesh is not particularly nutritious, it is a light and agreeable article of food; and none but those who have lived in the country, and have received the unexpected visit of friends to dinner, can form an adequate idea of the convenience of having a plump rabbit or two at hand in the hutch.

But we hold that, besides their material profitableness, there is a moral value attached to these animals. They afford an early lesson to the young of the responsibility of having live animals to feed and tend. Their proprietorship affords an opportunity of exercising the priceless qualities, in after-life, of thrift, attentiveness, good management, forbearance, and forethought. Innocent and unfailing amusement is thus derived from the daily practice of prudent habits, which are an excellent preparation for a subsequent charge of greater importance and difficulty.

The dung of these animals is an excellent manure for clayey soils, and is particularly serviceable in the culture of vines and fibrous-rooted green-house plants.

The rabbit shares with the fowl and the pig the merit of being a save-all,—being a transmuter of useless scraps and offal into useful and valuable fur and flesh. All sorts of vegetable tops and parings, weeds from the garden, which are not of too moist a nature—which would otherwise meet with no better fate than to be swept away to the rubbish-heap—will, with the addition of sufficient dry food, serve to maintain a little stud of rabbits. The cast-out refuse of three or four gardens, in a village, in the hands of many an ardent young stock-master, would serve, under a judicious administration, to rear, feed, and fatten his little flock. And in house-keeping, as well as in agriculture, trifling means of profit ought not to be neglected, when they are capable of being secured with only trifling exertion and the outlay of a small amount of capital, and especially when they are, as in this instance, the natural appendage of every poultry-yard or homestead which pretends to be of the least importance. The misfortune is, that exaggerated accounts have been given to the world which led to failures.

On the other hand, it is a false accusation to charge these animals with consuming any undue and enormous quantity of fodder. Some authors have asserted that ten rabbits will eat as much as a cow; but it seems to be proved that it would take at least fifty or sixty of them to effect so great a consumption as that. Probably the observers who have stated the fact, founded their calculations on the superfluous quantity of herbage which might have been supplied, and which the rabbits soon reduced to the state of filthy litter. The objection made to the unwholesomeness of rabbit-keeping, in consequence of the smell which their hutches emit if neglected, is equally applicable to any other breach of cleanly habits. The evil and the remedy are in the hands of those who made the complaint. The rabbit itself is naturally a cleanly animal, and when confined by itself will always choose one particular spot or corner in which to deposit its ordure, and will be careful not to defile any other.

The cottager, the only meat on whose table is often a morsel of salt pork, will not prove so hard to please when he sits down to a fine rabbit of his own rearing and fatting.

The food of the rabbit is entirely vegetable. They feed upon common grass, clover, lucern, and on good hay, pea and bean vines. Greens and roots form excellent food, and potatoes boiled or steamed. They will fatten on them, but still more if they are given oats or bran. Some think their flesh is less dry when fed chiefly upon succulent herbs; but with these moist foods they must always have a proportionable quantity of the dry food, as hay, bread and oats, bran, brewers' grains, chaff, and the like; or when they have greens, they must not have drink. At all times they drink but little. The test of health is their dung being not too moist.

"In England," says a writer in the *Cultivator*, "the rabbit formerly held the rank of 'farm-stock,' and thousands of acres were exclusively devoted to its production; families were supported, and rents, rates, and taxes were paid from its increase and sale. I remember visiting a farm of Lord Onslow's, in Surrey, containing about 1,400 acres. It was in the occupation of an eminent flock-master and agriculturist, who kept some hundreds of hutched rabbits for the sake of their manure, which he applied to his turnip crop; added to this, their skins and carcasses were quite an item of profit, notwithstanding the care of them required an old man and a boy, with a donkey and cart. The food used was chiefly brewers' grains, millers' waste, bran and hay, with clover and roots; the cost of keeping not exceeding two pence a week. The hutches stood under a long shed, open on all sides, for the greater convenience of cleaning and feeding. I was told that the manure was much valued by the market gardeners around London, who readily paid 2s. 6d. a bushel at the rabbitries. These rabbitries are very numerous in all the towns and cities of England, and form a source of amusement or profit to all classes, from the man of fortune to the day-laborer. Nor is it unfrequent that this latter produces a rabbit from an old tea-chest, or dry-goods box, that wins the prize from its competitor of the mahogany hutch or ornamental rabbitry."

NATURE AND HABITS.

EVERY class of stock-keeping and menagerie management, in order to be permanently successful, and not conducted at mere haphazard, must be founded on a previous knowledge of the habits and constitution of the creatures kept; and therefore, as we here desire to communicate all the information which a novice requires, we believe that the inexperienced breeder of rabbits will best understand the theory and principles of his art, if we first make him acquainted with the precise nature of the animal with which he proposes to deal.

"The rabbit belongs to that order of the class Mammalia, or suck-giving animals, which is called *Incisores*, because they *cut* their food with the front teeth of their upper and lower jaws. They do not grind it, like the horse, the ox, and the elephant, for the simple reason that they have no grinders, or molar teeth. Some of these "cutters" are carnivorous, or rather omnivorous, like the rat; others are herbivorous in general, but occasionally insectivorous, like the Guinea-pig (which the old French writers call the Connil d'Inde, or Indian rabbit); some, like the hare, feed exclusively on vegetables and grain; and the rabbit, unless under exceptional circumstances, belongs to this latter category. The rabbit and the Guinea-pig are the only "cutters" that have been strictly *domesticated* by man; though he has made pets of the squirrel, the dormouse, the marmot, the albino mouse, and one or two others."

The male rabbit is called "a buck," the female "a doe." "The English language has not, like the French, a special word (*lapereau*) to denote the young. Rabbits are polygamous—one male being quite sufficient for as many as thirty females; in warrens, only one is allowed to a hundred. The adult bucks are overbearing, mischievous, and quarrelsome. Success very much depends on the way in which they are managed; and consequently, rabbit-keeping is an amusement better adapted for boys than for girls, unless, indeed, they have an elder brother or parent who will take upon himself the entire direction of the breeding department."

BREEDING.

TAME rabbits are raised in hutches or boxes placed in apartments constructed on purpose for them, or in sheds. They may also be bred in small artificial warrens, prepared for them, where the soil is extremely dry, and well drained by a ditch all around it, and having banks raised for the rabbits to burrow in. A damp situation will be fatal to the stock. As the nature of the rabbit is to dig, care must be taken to sink the wall or fence sufficient to prevent them from undermining and making their escape.

The doe will breed at the age of a year, and sometimes at the age of six months, and her period of gestation is thirty or thirty-one days. But they should not be allowed to breed at that early age, as they are liable to abortion; and even if that misfortune is avoided, their little ones come into the world exceedingly weak, and sometimes defective. It cannot be expected to happen otherwise. Nature, in spite of all her efforts, will fail to develop at the same time the strength of the mother and of her off-spring also. The attempt will assuredly be made at the expense of one or the other—probably both. The young ones will have to suffer from an insufficient supply of milk; their constitution will prove weak and rickety; and the chances are, that they will die of debility before attaining an age to be of any use.

The doe goes with young thirty, or sometimes thirty-one days. A fortnight after she has littered, she is ready to visit the buck again, with whom she should be placed in the evening, and returned to her young the following morning. She *might* be put to him five or six days after bringing forth, as she is almost always in heat; but she requires a fortnight's repose to recover her strength. She breeds throughout the winter as well as in summer, and will, therefore, according to strict theory, produce eight litters in the course of a single year. But all this supposes every circumstance to be invariably favorable:— that she should be thoroughly well fed, never out of health, and that no untoward accident happen. A much safer calculation is to reckon upon six litters a year; some breeders are even contented with supposing five to be successfully reared. When the buck is not more than five or six years old, and the doe than five, it is very rare that she misses. But should it so happen, give her a nutritious and stimulating diet, such as parsley, celery, fennel, thyme, and other aromatic herbs, besides a liberal diet of oats, bran, or pollard, and sweet hay; keep her tolerably warm, and in a few days she will be all right again. After her night's absence, she will be returned to her own hutch, and will then suckle her last progeny another week longer. To keep all the parent animals in this constant state of isolation is one of the main and fundamental maxims of rabbit-keeping; for the buck will not only greatly harass the doe, if he is allowed free access to her, but will often kill the young while they are still blind and helpless.

The number at a birth varies from two or three up to eight and ten young ones. In general, the larger the breed, the fewer at a birth. As many as eighteen have been known in extreme cases. But eight or nine are a much better average. Some breeders prefer to have no more than five or six, and take away those that are in excess. When it can be done without too much disturbance, the plan is a good one, especially when the doe has lost or destroyed her former litters. Sometimes, when she is weak and exhausted at the time of littering, she feels that she can suckle only a limited number, she herself will save her owner the trouble of killing the supernumeraries, and will calculate according to her strength how many ought to be spared. But take six as the average number of little ones to be produced at each six litters, and we have thirty-six rabbits in the course of a twelvemonth as the produce of a single doe. More than that:—at six months old, the young rabbit is fully capable of becoming a parent in its turn. In two years, therefore, we should

have four successive generations of rabbits all the while
that the fecundity of the original ancestress is still going
on. "Rabbits," says Pennant, "will breed seven times
a year, and bring eight young ones each time." On a
supposition that this happens regularly during four years,
their numbers will amount to one million, two hundred
and seventy-four thousand, eight hundred and forty
head.

MANAGEMENT OF THE DOE.

THE intelligent breeder ought to know by his stud-book
(for he will give names to his favorites) the day on which
each doe is to bring forth. A few days beforehand, he
will throw into the hutch a large handful of coarse but
sweet hay. She will immediately make use of it to form
her nest, and will employ for the same purpose any
scraps, shreds, or odd bits that she can lay hold of. The
first outside structure arranged, she then strips off the fur
from beneath her belly, and devotedly denudes herself, to
secure a soft, warm couch for the reception of her expected
young. At this period, neglect may be fatal; she must
at the same time be kept quiet, and well fed, to support
her in nursing. The omission of a single meal may check
her milk, and occasion the death of several young. Few
things at this time are better for her than carrots and oats.
Wet vegetables are especially injurious. During the first
week, let her have plenty of bran, mingled with a little
salt.

If the doe has had a previous litter, they must all be removed before she brings forth a second time; her hutch, too, ought to have been well cleaned out. Take care not to touch the young; unless, at least, they are deposited in a wet place, or any of them die. All unnecessary disturbance or handling is apt to make the mother kill the whole of her family. When you find a doe overlays or eats her young, as they sometimes will, mark her well, and remember the circumstance; for should the same misfortune happen again, the best thing to be done is to fatten and kill her. If, however, she be a favorite animal, and an attempt at reformation be resolved upon, she must be abundantly fed with good substantial food, and disturbed no more than is absolutely necessary.

MANAGEMENT OF THE YOUNG.

THE little animals are born blind and helpless, covered only with a short velvety down. On the fifth day they open their eyes; on the sixth, the liveliest little fellows amongst them begin to peep outside the nest. At a month old they eat alone, and partake of food together with their mother. At six weeks old they no longer require the doe, and ought to be weaned. This short period is quite sufficient to allow to be spent in the first term of rearing them. If they were left longer, they would be apt to exhaust the dam, which ought to be avoided. After weaning, two modes of feeding have been adopted, with equal success:—the first is, to introduce all the weanlings, from time to time, into a large hutch or common apartment, in which they are tended carefully, kept warm and clean, and fed several times in the course of the day. At each feeding-time, every particle of victuals which has been trampled upon is scrupulously withdrawn; and it is found that, by observing these regulations, the losses are very few, or none. When two months and a half old, they will fatten on carrots, oats, hay, and bran, with a few peas now and then.

The second plan is to keep together all the young rabbits of the same month; that is to say, they are distributed in six large hutches or apartments, care being taken to

separate the males from the females (or to castrate them)
by the end of the third month. From the fifth to the
sixth month, all those intended for sale are disposed of,
after selecting the handsomest and best-tempered does to
serve as breeders. Does will continue prolific until they
are five years old. Beyond that age, it is rare to meet
with rabbits surviving in a domestic state. After that, it
is usual to fatten them for the table; though, in such
cases, the purchaser may complain that he has met with a
hard bargain. The duration of their natural life is said
to be from six to eight years. Buffon extends the term to
nine years.

HANDLING.

RABBITS are sometimes injured by being clumsily han-
dled. The proper way to take hold of them is, to grasp
the ears with the right hand, and to support the rump
with the left. To seize them by the leg is apt to dislocate
a limb, especially in the case of creatures that are shy;
an injudicious gripe round the neck or the body may
prove unexpectedly and suddenly fatal, by injury to the
vertebræ, compression of the lungs, or breaking of the
ribs; a hasty clutch at the tail may cause the fur of that
ornamental member to come off in one piece, and spoil
the animal's beauty for life. The instantaneous way in
which an adroit hand will kill a rabbit, apparently by the
merest touch, gives a forcible hint as to the caution we should
use in allowing a favorite animal to be captured and pulled

about by inexperienced persons. For does with young, the greatest tenderness is indispensable.

FEEDING.

RABBITS should be fed twice a day—at morning and at night. If on green food, it ought to be thoroughly dry before it is put into their racks or thrown upon the floor of their hutches. This diet would principally consist of the refuse of the garden vegetables, taking care to give only a moderate quantity of cabbages, lettuce, and all other cold and watery plants. Wet herbage is *deadly poison* to rabbits. The leaves and roots of carrots, all sorts of leguminous plants, the leaves and branches (or the prunings) of all kinds of trees, cabbage leaves, wild succory, parsley, &c., may be the diet of rabbits during summer. The great point, however, at all seasons, is to make the dry preponderate over the moist.

According to Mowbray, it is better to feed three times than twice a day. The art of feeding rabbits with safety and advantage, is always to give the preponderance to dry and substantial food. Their nature is congenial with that of sheep, and the same kind of food, with little variation, agrees with both. He contends that all weeds and the refuse of vegetation should be banished from rabbit feeding: such articles being too washy and diuretic, and can never be worth attention whilst the more solid and nutritious productions of the field may be obtained in such plenty, and will return so much greater profit. Rabbits which have as much oats as they will eat, can never take any harm from being indulged with almost an equal portion of good substantial vegetables. However, the test of their health is that their dung be not too moist.

Mr. E. E. Platt, of Albany, a successful breeder of lop-eared rabbits, informs us that he feeds brewers' grains, and finds them the best and most economical feed for winter; and, contrary to the natural supposition, they do not sour in the least, and their bowels are kept in good order. The grain proper for rabbits is oats, peas, wheat, pollard, and some give buckwheat; the greens and roots, the same as our cattle or sheep crops; viz., carrots, parsnips, rutabaga, artichokes, and potatoes, if baked or steamed; lucern, cabbage leaves, clover, tares, pea and bean haulm. The best dried herbage is clover and meadow hay, and pea and bean straw.

"In relation to feeding," says a writer in the *Cultivator*, over the signature of "R," who is good authority in such matters, "I would caution breeders not to use lettuce after the plant begins to put up its seed stalks, as its narcotic effect is then so strong as to cause death. I lost in one summer over twenty rabbits from this plant before discovering the cause. Corn, sown broadcast, affords an abundant and an excellent substitute. I think the rutabaga, as a winter vegetable, is generally preferred to carrots. Water, I find, may be given to rabbits when six months old without any ill effects, though so positively interdicted by all the 'fancy.' I have not heretofore sufficiently enforced the importance of a *liberal* supply of hay, which, in winter, affords the rabbit that amount of bulk necessary to the healthy feeding of all animals, and which oats alone would not give. It matters not how coarse the hay, nor how full

2

of trash and weeds, it will be equally sought, and sometimes preferred to any grain, especially if the rabbit is a little off its feed."

A *variety* of food is a great thing; and, surely, the fields, and gardens, and hedges furnish this variety—all sorts of grasses, strawberry leaves, and ivy. They should have oats once a day. When the doe has young ones, feed her most abundantly with all sorts of greens and herbage, and with carrots and other things mentioned before, besides giving her a few oats once a day. But do not think that, because she is a small animal, a little feeding or a little care is sufficient. To those gentlemen who keep rabbits for the use of their family, (and a very useful and convenient article they are too,) I would observe, that if they find their rabbits die, they may depend on it that ninety-nine times out of the hundred *starvation* is the malady.

"It is a matter of surprise to an American first visiting England," remarks L. F. Allen, in his "Rural Architecture," "to see the quantities of game which abound at certain seasons of the year in London and other markets of that country, in contrast of the scanty supply, or rather no supply at all, existing in the markets of American cities. The reason for such difference is, that in England, Scotland, Wales, and Ireland, every acre of the soil is appropriated to some profitable use, while we, from the abundance of land in America, select only the best for agricultural purposes, and let the remainder go barren and uncared for. Lands appropriated to the rearing of game, when fit for farm pasturage or tillage, is unprofitable, generally, with us; but there are thousands of acres barren for other purposes, that might be devoted to the breeding and pasturage of rabbits, and which, by thus appropriating them, might be turned to profitable account. All the preparation required is, to enclose the ground with a high and nearly close paling fence, and the erection of a few rude hutches inside for winter shelter and the storage of their food. They will burrow into the ground, and breed with great rapidity; and in the fall and winter seasons, they will be fat for market with the food they gather from the otherwise worthless soil over which they run. Rocky, bushy, and evergreen grounds, either hill, dale, or plain, are good for them, wherever the soils are dry and friable. The rabbit is a gross feeder, living well on what many grazing animals reject, and gnawing down all kinds of brush, briars, and noxious weeds.

"The common domestic rabbits are probably the best for market purposes, and were they to be made an object of attention, immense tracts of mountain in New Jersey, Pennsylvania, New York, and New England, could be made available for this object.

"Some may think," continues Mr. Allen, "this a small business. So is making pins, and rearing chickens and bees. But there are an abundance of people whose age and capacity are just fitted for it, and for want of other employment are a charge upon their friends and the public."

On the subject of rearing "Fancy Rabbits," and their necessary accommodations, we subjoin the following from the pen of Mr. F. Rotch, of Morris, Otsego county, N. Y., who imported the first of the large lop-eared rabbits into this country, some twelve or fourteen years ago. His beautiful and high-bred animals have occasionally been

exhibited at the fairs of the State Agricultural Society,
for which premiums have been awarded and the highest
commendations elicited.

"Rabbits kept for profit in the vicinity of a city, and
where there are mills, may be raised at a very small cost;
and when once known as an article of food, will be liberally paid for by the epicure, for their meat is as delicate
as a chicken's, and their fat mild and very rich.

"I am surprised they are not more generally kept as a
source of amusement, and for the purpose of experiment.

"There is, I think, in many, a natural fondness for animals, but not easily indulged without more room than is often
to be found in city residences. Fowls and pigeons trespass
on our neighbors, and are a frequent cause of trouble.
This objection does not hold good against a rabbit, which
occupies so small a space, that where there is an out-house
there may be a rabbitry. English children are encouraged
in their fondness for animals, as tending to good morals
and good feelings, and as offering a home amusement, in
contradistinction to street associations.

"In England, and in other parts of Europe, a love for
animals, with the attendance and personal care necessary
to their comfort, is encouraged from childhood up, as having a beneficial influence on the character.

"The operatives, mechanics, and laborers in other countries seem to have a perfect passion for such pursuits, and
take the greatest interest and pride in breeding and perfect-
ing the lesser animals, though often obliged to toil for the
very food they feed to them. Here, too, home influences
are perceived to be good, and are encouraged by the em-

ployer, as supplying the place of other and much more questionable pursuits and tastes.

"In relation to the man of leisure and science, I would remark, that as the artist delights in the power of moulding the inert clay into life-like form, so does the intelligent and amateur breeder find infinite pleasure in the higher and more difficult art of modelling the live material into its most symmetrical proportions. And why should there not be as much satisfaction in producing what is excellent on a small, as on a large scale? Is not the statuette as beautiful, and is it not as much an effort of genius and art as the statue?

"To myself," continues Mr. R, "the rabbitry is a 'studio,' whereof the material is cheap, rapidly produced, soon perfected, very abundant, and occupying a small space, and is thus brought under my own immediate care and observation, with but little trouble, requiring months only instead of years, to *practically test* theories and speculations, and for studying some of the most important, but not understood, laws of nature. Such as, how far it may be safe to use close affinities? And if deteriorating, what are the first and warning symptoms? In what order does the animal structure give way under a persisted course of such breeding? The same as to cross-breeding, and how far the control of the breeder is diminished by its continuance? The comparative influence of the parents on the offspring, and how evinced? These, and many other unsettled questions involving the first principles of breeding, would require almost a lifetime to decide by experiments on the larger animals, to say nothing of the large outlay it would require, and the serious losses that might reasonably be expected to attend it."

With all due appreciation of the very important assist-ance rendered the agriculturist by analytical chemistry, I would sooner trust the practical experiments of the rab-bitry as to the value of the different kinds of food, than I would the analysis of the laboratory! And though one may prove that a bushel of rutabaga be little more or less than a pail of water, yet if the other showed me that tur-nips, as the principal food, with but two ounces of hay per day to the rabbit, developed the animal frame by a healthy growth, an abundance of muscle and some fat, I should be strongly tempted to pour out the water and pour in the turnips.

"Clubs and societies abound for the breeding and exhibi-tion of the 'Fancy-Lops,' now the favorite rabbit in England, and originally imported from Madagascar. Much pains have been taken, and much money spent, to bring them to their present perfection in form, color, and size; all of which are minutely attended to, and not very easily combined in any one animal, and hence they form an admirable test of skill on the part of the breeder.

"For instance, a rabbit, to come out a winner at one of those exhibitions, must possess all the points of symmetry in common with the larger animals of the improved breed; such as a small, clean head, wide and full shoul-, ders, broad and deep chest, a wide back, large loin, full quarters, and fine bone.

"Some of us, I suspect, find it no easy matter to get even thus far in the catalogue of excellences; but to all

these essentials are to be added the more *conventional,* and
perhaps the more difficult points, of beauty and fancy, as
laid down by the various societies; embracing not only
form and color, but the particular disposition and forms
of color.

"A prize rabbit, then, must possess, besides the before-
mentioned properties, a full, round, clear eye, an ear (colored as the body) long and broad, of a soft, delicate tex-
ture, dropping alike, and nearly perpendicularly, down by
the side of the cheek, with the convex of the ear turned
rather out than in. This is termed its '*earage.*' The color
on the body must be in strong, rich, unbroken masses,
spreading itself uniformly over the back, sides, and
haunches, called the '*saddle,*' but breaking into spots and
patches on the shoulders, known as the '*chain.*' The
head must be full of color, interspersed with white on the
forehead and cheeks, while the darker marking on the
point of the nose, and on each lip, goes by the name of
the '*butterfly,*' from the resemblance it should bear to
that insect. Add to all this a large, full dew-lap, beautifully white, which spreads itself (when the animal reposes)
over the fore feet, and forms a rich cushion for the head.
All this, combined, would indeed form a perfect lop-eared
rabbit, worthy to enter, and likely to win the prize collar,
be it of gold or silver; and the breeder may be proud of
his success, though it be but a rabbit. Much consequence
is attached to the length, quality, and carriage of the *ear,*
in awarding premiums. I was indifferent to this point of
length, and purchased much lower in consequence, paying
from ten to forty shillings sterling apiece for those I imported, according to age and quality; whereas five guin-

2*

eas is not an uncommon price; and individuals have been
sold as high as thirty guineas! The consequence of my
selection is, that out of fifty rabbits, in my rabbitry, I
have not one that will exceed eighteen inches length of
ear from point to point! Whereas the *Illustrated News*
of May, 1850, gave portraits of the two prize rabbits at
the Rochester Show, from the excellent stud of Mr. George
Tavell, measuring in length of ear 21¾ inches and 21¼
inches, and nearly five inches wide."

"The usual colors are black, blue, gray, yellow, and
tortoise-shell, on white grounds. These are called '*broken
colors;*' when not mixed with either, they are termed
'*selfs.*'"

"The rabbit easily conforms itself to the means, condition, and circumstances of its owner: occupies but little
space, breeds often, comes early to maturity, and is, withal,
a healthy animal; requiring, however, to be kept clean,
and to be *cautiously* fed with *succulent* food, which must
always be free from dew or rain. Water is unnecessary
for them when fed with 'greens.'"

"To does, when suckling, I give what they will eat of
both green and dry food. The cost to me is about three
cents a head per week."

"My young rabbits, when taken from the doe, say at
eight or ten weeks old, are turned out together till about
six months old, when it becomes necessary to take them
up and put them in separate hutches, to prevent their
fighting and destroying each other. The doe at that age
is ready to breed; her period of gestation is about thirty-
one days, and she produces from three or four to a dozen
young at a 'litter.' It is not well to let her raise more

than six, or even four, at a time—the fewer, the larger and finer the produce."

Young rabbits are killed for the table at any age from twelve weeks to twelve months old, and are a very acceptable addition to the country larder.

"Hutches are made singly, or in stacks, to suit the apartments, which should be capable of thorough ventilation. The best size is, probably, about three feet long, though some recommend four feet, two feet deep, and fourteen inches high, with a small apartment partitioned off from one end, nearly a foot wide, as a breeding-place for the doe. A wire door forms the front, and an opening is left behind for cleaning; the floor should have a descent to the back of the hutch of two inches. All edges should be tinned, to save them from being gnawed."

RABBIT COURTS.

"PERHAPS the most pleasing, and, for the animals, the most healthy place to keep rabbits in, is a paved yard. If well situated, it becomes, in fact, a practical realization, on a small scale, of Olivier De Serres' grand idea. Two sides of the court-yard may be bounded by tall buildings, as houses or stabling; if they stand to the north and east, so much the better. The other two sides should consist of a wall not more than five feet high, to admit air and sunshine. For security from intrusion from without, and to confine any fowls that may be kept within, palings may be fixed to the top of these low walls, without any inconvenience arising. The great object is to have the court at once airy, sunshiny, sheltered, and secure. In one or two corners of the court, or against one or two of its sides, there should be thrown a broad heap of earth and rubbish, eighteen inches lower than the top of the wall. In this, the rabbits will burrow and amuse themselves—though it is better to prevent the does from nesting there, for fear of the attacks of cats and rats. The buck must be retained a close prisoner, in a box of his own. The breeding does, when their time of kindling approaches, will be comfortably settled in separate hutches, to be described hereafter. The day when each doe is to bring forth will be known from the stud-book, even if it is not indicated by the preparations she makes—

such as carrying about straws and haulms in her mouth, and biting them into separate lengths. The rest of the stock will associate indiscriminately together·in the court, with the sole exception that all males will be withdrawn, cut, or sent to the kitchen, as soon as they reach an age to prove troublesome; and that young ones just weaned, that is, from six to eight weeks old, will be kept in a hutch by themselves till they are strong enough to join the general herd.

The management of the rabbit court is obvious. Food, either dry or green, has only to be scattered about on the pavement of the court. The small proportion of individuals in confinement will, of course, require extra attention, which will demand no great time to fulfil properly. All that is necessary is, to do it regularly and unfailingly. Rabbits so kept are much more amusing objects than when they are constantly hidden from sight in their hutches. Their gambols are seen—their little antics with one another—their cleanly habits in brushing their fur coats—and even the petty quarrels and jealousies which arise from the elder ones striving for the mastery. They will also become so tame as to eat out of the hand, and to flock around their feeder when he enters with a bundle of vegetables or straw. The whole stud should be so liberally supplied with provender, that those intended to be eaten may be able to fatten upon it; the growing and the breeding rabbits will amply repay the share they consume of this liberal diet, by the rapidity with which they come to hand, and the strength and thriftiness of the litters they bring forth. A rabbit court like this is particularly convenient for consuming the refuse and sweepings of a large kitchen and flower-garden. We strongly recommend a rabbit court to those whose premises and situation allow of such a plan being adopted.

RABBIT PIT.

ANOTHER form of dwelling, imitating in some degree the natural habitation of the animal, though less so than the court, is the rabbit pit. One of this kind is described in "Farming for Ladies," and annexed we give a wood-cut from the sketch in that work. The enclosure was only about twelve feet in diameter, covering a pit of six feet in depth, in which the rabbits were confined, and through the sandy sides of which they burrowed to the extent of from ten to fourteen feet to make their nests. The proprietor, however, it was said, intended to fill up three feet of the depth, as he thought that the rabbits should be brought nearer to the air. The mode of catching the rabbits in the pit was with a long stick, forked at the end, which was hooked upon their neck when they came out to feed; or they were snared with a bit of wire fastened to the end of a stick.

We quote another rabbit pit from the *Agricultural Gazette:*—"In the Isle of Thanet, on the east coast of Kent, the writer witnessed and superintended, on his own property, the method which he now proceeds cursorily to describe, and the diagram on page 41 will tend to define the limits of the spaces required.

"No. 1 represents a pit five feet on each side of the square. It is an oblong, four feet long, and about two feet broad. Both are dug to the depth of six feet, perfectly

RABBIT PIT.

level at the bottom and sides, the latter so much wider
than the wooden curbs, as to admit of a facing of four-inch
brick-work, in cement, excepting the spaces to admit of
about six arched openings (as marked) of dimensions sufficient for the passage of the largest rabbit. 2, is the feed-

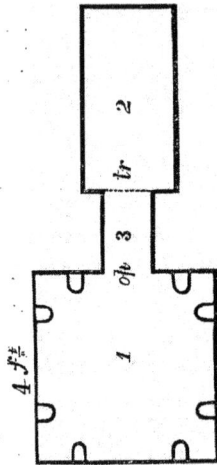

ing department. 3, is only an arched passage, tunnelled at
the ground level of the bottom of the two pits, about a foot
wide and broad, to serve as a communication between the
pits. This is also bricked and arched, but is not seen at the
top. A covering of oil cloth is added to the curb of each
pit, and the cloth extends over the frame several inches
beyond the curb, in order to prevent the entry of the
heaviest rain. At the place *op*, the arched passage is
always open; and so it is also at the other extremity,

marked *tr*, excepting only when any of the rabbits are to
be taken. Dryness is essential to the prosperity of this
animal, therefore the soil should not only be naturally dry,
but must be protected above, and kept secure at the sides
and bottoms of the pit by the best brick-work. From
what has been stated, it will be understood that a sound
gravelly or sandstone soil forms by far the most appropriate
medium for the warren, which the rabbits burrow into,
and excavate according to their own requirements. Four
does and a buck may be reckoned a good breeding stock;
and something of the kind was found when the writer
purchased the property."

The general idea of a rabbit pit being thus suggested,
it will be easy for an amateur to modify it at his pleasure.
Of the two specimens given, we would only observe that
they both appear too small in their dimensions. A pit,
also, is not a nice thing to have on one's premises. We
doubt whether animals kept constantly below the surface
of the ground would be maintained in such good health
as those above it. Undoubtedly, the most perfect arrangement would be a combination of the rabbit court with the
rabbit pit.

RABBIT HUTCHES.

WE now come to what appears the simplest of all matters, and which yet, if it be not well contrived, will have a most influential effect in causing failure. From a tea-chest to a worn-out portmanteau or a leaky tub, anything has been thought good enough to keep a rabbit in. "Everybody," says Cobbett, "knows how to knock up a rabbit hutch." If the rabbits themselves could only speak, they would tell us that many a body sets about it in bungling manner, and proves himself profoundly ignorant of the fundamental principles of rabbit architecture.

To learn these, we must go to the warren. There we find that the rabbit makes its dwelling in a sandy soil, and therefore well drained; in hillocks and mounds, in preference to hollow bottoms, and therefore dry. The burrows frequently communicate with each other, and therefore allow a certain amount of ventilation, the wind blowing into the mouth of the hole being often sufficient to insure that. The thick stratum of light earth which covers the habitations of a colony of rabbits, causes coolness in summer and warmth in winter. In the depth of a burrow it never freezes, and is never oppressively hot. In short, with the exception of the absence of light, which is of little importance in a *sleeping-place*, a rabbit's burrow, magnified to corresponding proportions, would make, at a pinch, a very bearable dwelling for human beings devoid of other shelter; the nest which a doe prepares for her young is soft and warm enough for a baby to lie in, if sufficiently enlarged. And in truth, many thousands of our fellow-creatures spend their lives, are born, and die, in cellars which are less wholesome than a rabbit's burrow on this large imaginary scale would be.

Whatever form of hutch, therefore, be adopted, it should be well sheltered, if possible; it should stand within another airy building, or at least under cover. Its temperature should never descend to the freezing point, nor mount beyond summer heat—scarcely so high, if it can be avoided. On this account, rabbit hutches, or cabins of brick-work, built in a court, offer many advantages; if made of wood, the material should be solid. Were we now to recommence rabbit-keeping, we would contrive a hutch whose top should be thatched with straw and reeds, to avoid all sudden chills, as well as bakings and broilings from the noontide sun. Of course, all sorts of drippings from eaves, draughts of air, and inundations from bad drainage, should be placed out of the possibility of annoying the rabbits. Many stocks, unfortunately, are constantly exposed to all these evils. Their owners then complain that they do not succeed, and lay all the fault of the failure to the poor, good - for - nothing, troublesome, and tender creatures.

"For this reason, hutches should never stand on the level of the ground; they should be raised at least a few inches (though a foot or two is better), either on legs or benches. The wood of which they are constructed ought to be thick, more for the sake of warmth than for strength;

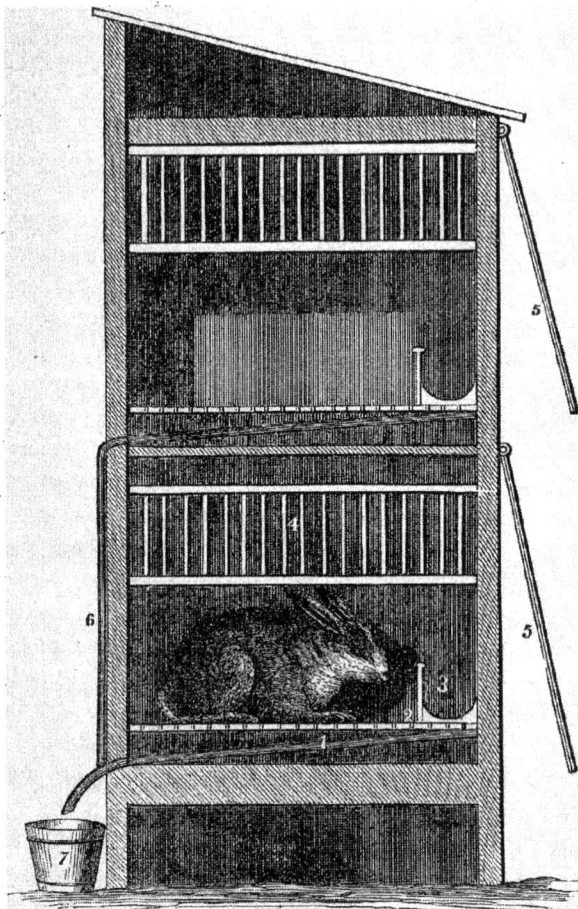

SECTION OF A TWO-TIER RABBIT HUTCH.

for if the rabbits do happen to gnaw them, ten to one it is
done more for the want of dry food and an irresistible
craving after it, than for mischief's sake. The dimensions
will vary according to circumstances, and every amateur
will suit his own convenience; but no hutch to contain a
single full-grown rabbit, ought to be less than a good yard
square in area. The depth is of less consequence.

We now give a wood-cut of a form of hutch which has
many advantages, and which is useful where a large stock
is kept, because. it is capable of being repeated to any
extent in length, like a row of houses, and also, as the
annexed figure shows, may be constructed with a couple of
stories or more. The first, or false bottom (2), is a frame-
work of strong splines, with a sufficient interval between
them to allow the urine and small fragments of offal to
pass through. About an inch beneath this first bottom is
a second (1), of wood, covered with zinc. It is fixed with
a gentle slope from back to front, to aid the escape of the
urine to the gutter, which will be conveyed to a pail (7)
by means of a tube (6), which communicates with the
inclined bottom of each hutch. This bottom ought to be
movable, slipping in a groove, in order that it may be
more easily cleansed. To avoid all likelihood of infection,
the bucket which receives the urine should be carefully
emptied twice a day, and well rinsed out; for the urine
of the rabbit is *the sole cause* of any offensive smell which
may emanate from a hutch. The door of the hutch (5) is
a frame of wire-work, suspended at the top by a couple of
hinges, and opening at the bottom. It is kept shut by a
hook or a button. Doors like these are easy to open, and
allow a convenient means of changing the litter, which

requires to be removed from time to time. If preferred, however, the door may go to slip in a groove, or to open at the side; but the former plan is altogether the best. Each hutch should be furnished with a little rack, fixed against one of the sides, to prevent the rabbits from wasting their food; for, like other of our domestic animals, they will reject the provender which they have once trodden and blown upon. In courts, a little rack on the model of a sheep rack is not only a pretty toy, but a useful article of furniture. At the back a little trough or manger should be fixed, to hold the bran and corn which is desirable for all, but more especially for nursing-does. The troughs for hutches in which weanling rabbits are kept should be very narrow, to prevent the little ones from getting into them.

Besides the hutches destined for does, there should be one of larger dimensions for the buck, not only to accommodate his robuster proportions, but to allow a doe to spend the night with him conveniently.

"This matter of rabbitry," observes Mr. Allen, in his "Rural Architecture," "and its various explanations, may be considered by the plain, matter-of-fact man, as below the dignity of people pursuing the *useful* and *money-making* business of life. Very possible. But many boys — for whose benefit they are chiefly introduced—and *men* even, may do worse than to spend their time in such apparent trifles. It is even better than going to a horse-race. It is better even than going to a trotting match, where *fast men*, as well as *fast* horses, congregate. It is better, too, than a thousand other places where boys *want* to go when they have nothing to interest them at home.

One half of the farmers' boys, who, discontented at home, leave it for something more congenial to their feelings and tastes, do so simply because of the excessive dulness and want of interest in objects to attract them there, and keep them contented. Those who have been well and indulgently, as well as methodically, trained, may look back and see the influence which all such little things had upon their early thoughts and inclinations; and thus realize the importance of providing for the amusements and pleasures of children in their early years. The dovecote, the rabbitry, the poultry-yard, the sheep-fold, the calf-pen, the piggery, the young colt of a favorite mare, the yoke of yearling steers, or a fruit tree which they have planted and nursed, and called it, or the fruit it bears, *their own*—anything, in fact, which they can call *theirs*—are so many objects to bind boys to their homes, and hallow it with a thousand nameless blessings and associations, known only to those who have been its recipients. Heaven's blessings be on the family homestead!"

We will now present the elevation and floor plan of Mr. Rodman's rabbitry, from Mr. Allen's work, together with the front and rear views of the hutches within them.

No. 1 is the gable end elevation of the building, with a door and window.

No. 2 is the main floor plan, or living-room for the rabbits.

EXPLANATION.—A, the doe's hutches, with nest boxes attached. B, hutches three feet long, with movable par-

No. I.—GABLE END ELEVATION.

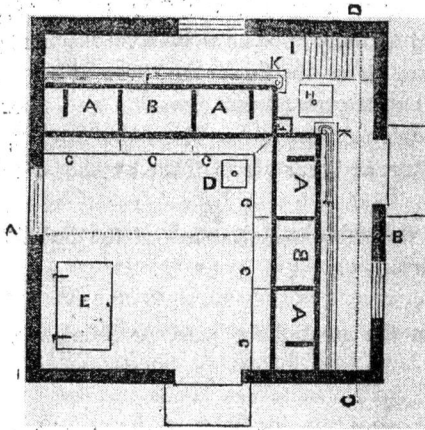

No. II.—MAIN FLOOR PLAN.

titions for the young rabbits; the two lower hutches are used for the stock bucks. C, a tier of grain boxes on the floor for feeding the rabbits—the covers sloping out towards the room. D, small trap-door, leading into the manure cellar beneath. E, large trap-door, leading into the root cellar. F, troughs for leading off urine from rear of hutches into the manure cellar at K, K. G, wooden trunk, leading from chamber above No. 3, through this into manure cellar. H, trap opening into manure cellar. I, stairs leading into loft No. 3, with hinged trap-door over head; when open, it will turn up against the wall, and leave a passage to clear out the hutches.

NOTE.—The grain boxes are one foot high in front, and fifteen inches at the back, with sloping bottoms and sloping covers. The floors of the hutches have a slope of two inches back. The hutches are furnished, at the back of the floor, with pieces of zinc, to keep them free from the drippings from above. The hutches are sixteen inches high, three feet long, and two feet deep.

The foregoing plans and explanations might perhaps be sufficient for the guidance of such as wish to construct a rabbitry for their own use; but as a complete arrangement of all the rooms which may be conveniently appropriated to this object, to make it a complete thing, may be acceptable to the reader, we conclude, even at the risk of prolixity, to insert the upper loft, and cellar apartments, with which we have been furnished; hoping that our youthful friends will set themselves about the construction of a branch of rural employment so home-attaching in its associations.

3

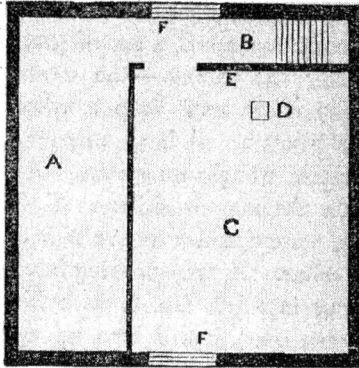

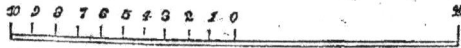

No. III.—LOFT, OR GARRET.

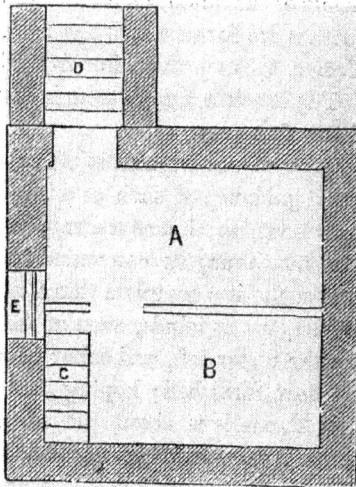

No. IV.—CELLAR.

No. 3 is the loft or chamber story, next above the main floor.

EXPLANATION.—A, place for storing hay. B, stairs leading from below. C, room for young rabbits. D, trap-door into trunk leading to manure cellar. E, partition four feet high. This allows of ventilation between the two windows, in summer, which would be cut off, were the partition carried all the way up.

No. 4 is the cellar under the rabbitry.

EXPLANATION.—A, manure cellar. B, root cellar. C, stairs leading to first, or main floor. · D, stairs leading outside. E, window—lighting both rooms of cellar.

No. 5 is a front section of rabbit hutches, eight in number, two in a line, four tiers high, one above another, with wire-screened doors, hinges, and buttons for fastening. A, the grain trough, is at the bottom.

No. 6 is the floor section of the hutches, falling, as before mentioned, two inches from front to rear. A, is the door to lift up, for cleaning out the floors. B, is the zinc plate, to carry off the urine and *running* wash of the floors. C, is the trough for carrying off this offal into the manure cellars, through the trunk, as seen in No. 2.

No. 7 is a rear section of hutches, same as in No. 5, with the waste trough at the bottom leading into the trench before described, with the cross section, No. 8, before described in No. 6.

A, a grated door at the back of the hutch, for ventilation in summer, and covered with a thin board in winter.

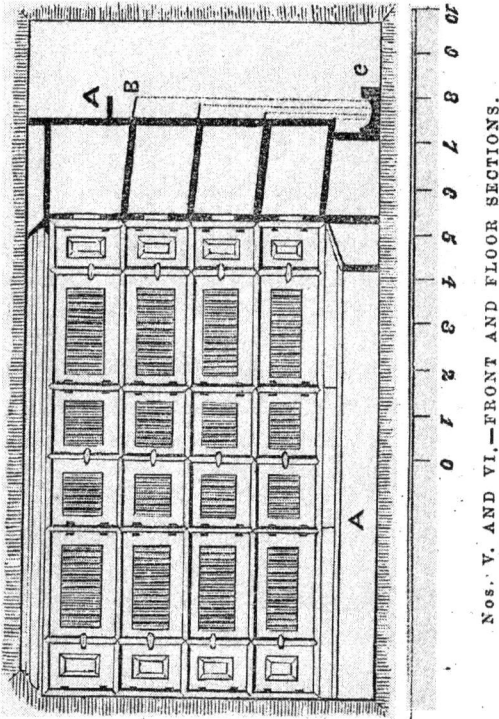

Nos. V. AND VI.—FRONT AND FLOOR SECTIONS.

B, a flap-door, four inches wide, which is raised for cleaning out the floor; under this door is a space of one inch, for passing out the urine of the rabbits. C, are buttons for fastening the doors. D, the backs of the bed-rooms, without any passage out on back side.

When rabbits are kept on a large scale, the hutches are assembled in one inclosure or building, which should be

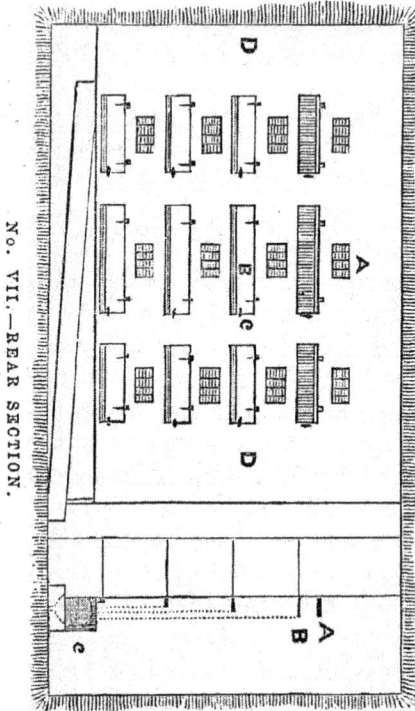

No. VII.—REAR SECTION.

covered with a roof and surrounded with walls to secure it from the weather, and the depredations of cats, rats, and other vermin. It is desirable that the inclosure be paved with square tiles;- which should have their joints well closed with cement, in order to prevent all leakage of urine or slops beneath the pavement. This accident is one of the causes most likely to engender disease amongst the stock. The reason is plain: the earth on which the pavements rest becomes sodden with liquid filth, an unpleasant smell is constantly exhaled, and whatever cleanliness may be observed above ground, beneath is a fertile source of epidemic maladies, which will go on increasing from month to month, and will sooner or later cause serious injury. In this inclosure rows of hutches are ranged one or more stories high. The first row will touch the wall; a passage will be left between that and the next row, and so on, till the inclosure is full, when you have a series of parallel passages and rows of hutches, allowing free ventilation and easy access of the persons who tend them.

In such an establishment, a constant renewal of air is a matter of the first necessity, which may be insured by fixing in the wall small grated windows opposite each other. If unpleasant smells are perceived, on entering in the morning, it is a hint to the rabbit-keeper to look to his litter and his ventilation. Hutches that are too small and too closely crowded together—that are cold and damp, or dirty and fœtid—are sufficient in themselves to bring on all the diseases to which rabbits are liable. Their result is loss of health, ophthalmia, want of appetite, diarrhœa, pot-belly, rot, mange and death. In the first stage of these disorders, something may be done by vigorous sanitary measures of cleanliness and ventilation, with judicious feeding and disinfection by means of chloride of lime. Rabbits are naturally of a robust constitution, and are but slightly liable to be attacked by small ailments; but when

they do become diseased, we may be sure that the evil is
of serious consequence.

We next give the figure of an independent hutch with
two apartments, which has been found very useful to contain a doe and her weanling young, before they are old
and strong enough to join the other fatting rabbits in the
court. It is also useful for the young beginner who is
making his first trial with two or three half-grown individuals of the sort of which he fancies. It is easily moved
under shelter or into the open air, easily tended and cleaned
out, and not costly to make.

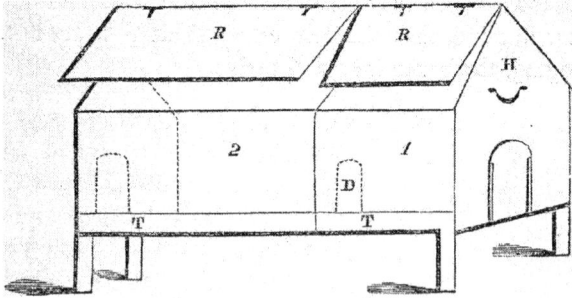

TWO-ROWED HUTCH.

Nos. 1 and 2 are the drainers, the second twice as large
as the first, communicating with a sliding-door D, which
can be opened or shut at pleasure. At each end is also a
door. The roof R, R, in separate pieces, is on one side a
wooden lid, moving on hinges at the top, and available
either to put in food or hay, or to catch the animals within.
T, T, are small troughs in front, for the reception of oats,

pollard, or peas. A little rack may be added at the back part; and an iron handle at each end, or at H, will enable a couple of persons to lift it from place to place with ease. It stands upon legs to raise it from the damp ground, and to keep mice from getting in and stealing the grain. The floor is pierced with holes to let the urine escape; other ordure can be removed through the gap at the bottom, into which the troughs are inserted, and which may also be contrived to admit a false bottom, like that of a bird-cage, but perforated, which every morning may be cleaned and scraped, besides being sprinkled with sand or straw. The dimensions of this hutch will greatly depend upon the room which the amateur has at command; but he will bear in mind, that the less cramped his pets are in their lodging, the better they will thrive.

SELECTION OF STOCK.

HOW TO COMMENCE RABBIT-BREEDING.

WE again call to our aid the little treatise on the rabbit of Mr. Delamer.

"To begin rabbit-keeping," says the author, "there are two modes of obtaining stock, which the amateur has the choice of adopting." This is in England. "The first plan is to purchase full-grown animals, a buck and as many does as may be required, and to let them breed once. Some persons are so little disposed to wait for the produce, that they will buy a doe or two far advanced with young, in order to see her progeny arrive as early as possible into the world. The second mode is to obtain one or two litters of young rabbits, after they are fairly weaned, at about nine or ten weeks old, and to tend them, and keep them, and to feed them up, till they are arrived at an age capable of being productive. Having ourselves repeatedly tried these two modes at different times of our life, we unhesitatingly recommend the second for preference, for the following reasons :—

In the first place, whoever sets about keeping any species of domestic bird or animal for the first time, will have a great many little details to learn, which will be most easily acquired by the observation of individuals sufficiently

3*   (57)

advanced in life to do without the care of their parents,
and also immature as not to require quite yet the fulfilment
of the great law of nature,—"increase and multiply."
There will be nothing beyond themselves to attend to.
We need only hint at the many points of health, dirt, habits, and peculiarities both of breeds, individuals, and sexes,
with which the amateur will thus become practically
acquainted, and which will render him more competent
for the management of his pets when they come to have
offspring in their turn. It is also a more economical plan,
requiring less outlay, and less liable to loss. Quite young
rabbits, of any ordinary kinds, can be bought both on the
continent and in England for a few shillings. In case of
failure, deaths are of less consequence; in the event of
success, superabundant males, and ugly and unpromising
·females, will always be useful to make their appearance on
the table. But to buy full-grown does that have already
reared two or three litters, of handsome appearance, and
probably the favorites of their owner, the purchaser must
expect to open his purse-strings, especially if he applies to
a respectable dealer; a disrespectable one might possibly
sell him, at a low price, a doe, which, though a good-look-
ing animal, may have some unseen but serious defect;
such as an invincible propensity to eat her young, or lurk-
ing symptoms of pot-belly and rot. Another point should
not be forgotten: some does, which have proved excellent
mothers with their old master, if changed to fresh quarters
(particularly if they have to travel far) when near their
time of kindling, and tended upon by unaccustomed hands,
and gazed at by strange faces, will *not* do well in their
new abode. They are apt to make an imperfect nest, to

neglect their young, and even to kill them; and this habit once begun, is ever afterwards to be apprehended.

All these various mishaps, which have disgusted many a young beginner, are avoided by stocking the court or the hutches with young individuals, which can be selected from, thinned out, or exchanged, till the amateur has got a stud to his mind. All the males, be it observed, must be secluded as soon as they are four or five months old.

If, after the foregoing caution, it be still determined to begin with a stock of full-grown animals, the points to be insisted on are, in the doe, teats visibly in a healthy and natural state, plump and swelled with milk if the term of pregnancy is advanced, or she has already littered; the head, with reference to the length of the muzzle and the breadth and development of the occiput, should form a sort of wedge; ears long, broad, and fine; chest expanded; legs strong, and wide apart. As far as profit and fecundity are concerned, a doe ought to bring forth not less than eight at each birth on an average. If she constantly produces less, it will be advisable to change her, even although she may be young and in good health; for it is an acknowledged fact that all individuals are not equally suited for reproduction.

The buck is at his best from one to five years of age; the doe, from eight months to four years: of course, care will be taken to see that they are not pot-bellied. Hard and well-pelleted dung is a certain indication of good health. It would be very convenient if there were unfailing signs, as in oxen, sheep, and horses, by which the exact age of a rabbit, up to a given period, could be ascertained; but all that can be done is, to distinguish vaguely an old one from a young one. The least equivocal symptoms of old age are, the general solidity and thickness of the skeleton, especially at the joints, as far as they can be felt by handling; the development of the belly to a considerable amount of obesity; and finally, the length and thickness of the nails.

Breeding does, when kept in hutches, are much better each in a hutch to herself, than inhabiting one common dwelling, however roomy it may be. When a number of does live in the same hutch, the consequences are sometimes quite as unfortunate as if the buck were in company with them. If a doe kindles, and leaves her little ones a moment to feed, the other does immediately crowd round the nest, through an instinct of curiosity, peep into, and not seldom disturb it with their fore paws. The mother rushes up to drive the other does away; a battle ensues; and half the little rabbits are either killed or wounded for life. The pregnant does which take part in these skirmishes, generally suffer abortion in consequence of their excitement, and the blows which they give and receive in the combat. Their owner may read the Riot Act afterwards, but the mischief is done.

VARIETIES OF RABBITS.

THE Rabbit is thought to have been originally a native of Spain, but has been common in the rest of Europe for ages. By domestication the colors of this species, as of all others which have been reclaimed by man, are very various: some individuals being black, blue, yellow, white, gray, lead color, and mixed in blotches of black and white, blue and white, &c.; one variety, called the Angora Rabbits, is furnished with long silky hair, something like the Angora Goat.

The wild rabbits are only mentioned here to warn the reader against supposing that *their* young, if caught at an early age, will be of any use to bring up in a domestic state. Of all the troublesome tasks a rabbit-fancier can undertake, is the attempt to rear a nest of young rabbits which have been taken from the warren, the field, or the down. We speak on this matter from experience. The difference of disposition is so immense and radical, that practical people are inclined to believe the two races to be derived from a distinct stock and origin. "Fancy rabbits," says Mr. Rogers, in his useful little treatise, "are not, as is generally supposed, the result of an improvement in the English breed of rabbits; but were originally brought from Tartary, Persia, and Asia Minor; and have been made the means of improving the domestic breeds in this country.

They require more warmth than the common English domestic rabbits; and thrive best when kept in an atmosphere the warmth of which varies from temperate to summer heat."

Domestic rabbits may be divided into four general leading varieties: the *Small Common Tame Rabbits*, the *Large Tame Rabbits*, the *Lop-eared sorts*, and the *Angolas*. Between each of these there are numerous half-breeds. Angora rabbits are distinguished by having long silky hair; their colors are mostly either pure white, or a mixture of black and white, or gray and white. Their fur is valuable when the skins can be obtained in considerable quantity; but they are delicate in constitution, less prolific, and many prejudiced persons object to eating them, because, they ,say, they resemble cats. Notwithstanding which, Angora rabbits are very pretty creatures, and well deserve the attention of those who think more about beauty and amusement than profit. We once saw, some fifteen years since, quite a large number of these beautiful little Angora Rabbits, in a yard of the late H. Watson, Esq., of New Windsor, near Hartford, Conn. They were very tame and quiet, and made quite a handsome show.

The *common small farm rabbits* are the nearest in size and appearance to the warren sorts. These are black, white, parti-colored, blue or slate colored, and brown or wild colored. They are hardy and prolific, suited for people living in a blustering climate, with only a limited supply of provender at command; they suffer less from neglect than the others,—though the less of that misfortune they have to undergo, the better. They are cheaper to buy, and, in short, are just the stock for a boy to begin

ANGOLA RABBIT.

with, till his experience entitles him to aspire to keep the fancy breeds. On the table, their flavor is as good as any, though they make a less magnificent dish when served up whole.

The large variety of tame rabbit is colored much the same as the former, except that it is more likely to produce *albinos,*—white individuals, with no coloring pigment in their eyes, and thence called "red-eyed" rabbits, because the blood circulating in the fine transparent vessels gives them that tint. White lop-eared rabbits in general have black eyelids and common eyes. With skilful management and liberal feeding, the large variety may be made to attain the weight of twenty pounds. That, or a trifle over, is the maximum. French Flanders has long been celebrated for, and still produces, admirable specimens of this variety. It can hardly be called a fancy rabbit, since it has not the lop ears which distinguish those breeds. It is merely an exaggeration or an enlargement of the smaller kind, though an accurate eye will observe that the proportions of its form are somewhat more elongated.

THE LOP-EARED RABBIT.

· HALF LOP

(68)

FANCY RABBITS.

LOP-EAR RABBITS.

THE lop-ear rabbits are the kinds which fanciers delight o revel in. The ears, instead of rising from the head, vith a tendency and inclination backward, like the comnon or wild variety, fall more or less to the side, as if hey had been folded and pressed down artificially, formng, more or less, decidedly pendant ears. Some few rarieties of goats and sheep exhibit a similar malformaion, for so it may be fairly called.

In rabbits, the first approximation to this peculiarity is hown by the *half-lop,* where one ear falls downwards or rontwise, and the other remains in its natural position, as een in the Frontispiece. The difference in the ears is very insightly, and is a great blemish in a fancier's eye; because he ears of all fancy rabbits ought to be exactly alike, oth in their shape, and in the way they point or fall.)therwise, it is as if a man had one short arm and one ong one, or one half of his face with a different sort of ountenance from the other half; and yet, a half-lop doe, f her other qualities are good, is not to be hastily dis-

carded; because she may, if judiciously coupled, produce
a few approved specimens in almost every litter. For it
is curious that, with fancy rabbits, when both the parents
are perfectly formed, have model ears, and are handsomely
marked, their progeny do not invariably turn out the
same; while from imperfect parents, if they have good
blood in their veins, there is a considerable chance of rearing at least a small number of superior young. Rabbit-
breeding, in such a case, acquires the same sort of interest
as the florist enjoys when he hopes to find in a bed of
seedling dahlias or carnations a first-rate specimen or two,
that shall reward him for all his patience and expense.
Still, the chances of success are greater when both the
parents have the desired characteristics.

The *oar-lop* is the next stage of deflection, when the
ears extend horizontally outwards on each side, forming
a line that is more or less straight, giving the idea of a
pair of oars which a waterman is resting out of the water
in his row-locks, while having a gossip as he is sculling
along. The term "oar-lop" is sufficiently descriptive.

The *horn-lop* rabbit has ears which descend obliquely
from the sides of the head, somewhat like the "cow with
the crumpled horn," in the immortal "House that Jack
built."

Flat-lops are the most natural, and therefore the most
perfect and valuable, rabbits, in a fancier's estimation.
The ears of the animal, instead of pointing upwards and
backwards, take a sudden turn downwards and forwards,
immediately from the crown of the head.

(The *dew-lap* is a point not to be neglected in the appearance of a fancy rabbit. It is sometimes compared to the

DEWLAP RABBIT.

dew-lap of a bull, or to the pendant skin, hardly to be called a pouch, which hangs under the chin in the African goose; but is really more like the double chin one sometimes sees ornamenting the neck of a well-fed old gentleman, or a full-blown matron, whose circumstances are easy, and whose labors are slight. It has the appearance of a *goitre*, without its unseemliness,—though goitred ladies are not without their admirers. The rabbit looks as if it had put on a fur tippet of the same material as its own, by way of a comforter, serving also as a cushion for the chin to rest upon, when "Bunny" is enjoying its afternoon's doze. A thick dew-lap is considered a great beauty and recommendation, but it is only slightly visible till the animal has arrived at its adult state.

MARKINGS: THE SMUT AND THE CHAIN−CARRIAGE.

OTHER points in fancy rabbits are more conventional and variable, and depend more upon individual taste. Peculiarities which are the rage to-day, may be only coldly looked upon to-morrow. Amongst these are those varieties of the animal which are discriminated by the combination of colors respectively belonging to them. We quote a paragraph from Mr. Rogers:—

"The fur of fancy rabbits may be blue, or rather lead-color and white, or black and white, or tawny and white, that is, tortoise-shell-colored. But it is not of so much importance what colors the coat of a rabbit displays, as it is that those colors should be arranged in a particular

4

manner, forming imaginary figures, or fancied resemblan-
ces of certain objects. Hence the peculiarities of their
markings have been denoted by distinctive designations.
What is termed the "blue butterfly smut" was for some
time considered the most valuable of fancy rabbits. It is
thus named on account of having bluish or lead-colored
spots on either side of the nose, considered as having
some resemblance to the spread wings of a butterfly, what
may be termed the groundwork of the rabbit's face being
white. A black and white rabbit may also have the face
marked in a similar manner, constituting a "black butterfly smut."

"But a good fancy rabbit must likewise have other
marks, without which it cannot be considered as a perfect
model of its kind. There should be a black or blue
patch of fur on its back, called the saddle; the tail must
be of the same color with the back and snout; while the
legs should be all white; and there ought to be dark
stripes on both sides of the body in front, passing backwards to meet the saddle, and uniting on the top of the
shoulders, at the part called the withers in a horse. These
stripes form what is termed 'the chain,' having somewhat the appearance of a chain or collar hanging round
the neck.

"The beauty and consequent worth of a fancy rabbit,
however, depend a good deal on its shape, or what is termed
its 'carriage.' A rabbit is said to have a good carriage
when its back is finely arched, rising full two inches above
the top of its head, which must be held so low as for the
muzzle and the points of the ears to reach almost to the
ground."

SALABLE VALUE.

Mr. Rogers says:—"The price of a fancy rabbit, like that of any other curiosity, must depend upon its displaying more or less qualities which have been considered as constituting the perfection of its kind. Considerable sums have no doubt been sometimes paid for particularly fine specimens of fancy rabbits. Well-bred rabbits may frequently be purchased at reasonable rates when young; and if well tended and managed, they may afterwards prove very valuable." Prize rabbits have been sold at five pounds sterling; and even eighteen guineas have been paid for a prize rabbit.

"To all this," says *R.*, in the *Cultivator*, "I am well aware, the question will arise with many of your readers— *Cui bono?* And the conclusion as definitively follow— '*It won't pay.*' Perhaps not; and yet I believe that were things tried on a small scale, and a small club formed for the purpose of exhibition and experiment, that it would become, to its members, a source of much more interest than they could now suppose. As opportunities will now become numerous of purchasing rabbits from the best London breeders, I will give you the following names:— Dr. Handy, just over Waterloo Bridge; Mr. Payne, 142 White Chapel; Mr. Bailey, of the Star Coffee-House, Union street, out of Bishopsgate; Mrs. Webster, Pleasant

Place, Stamford street, Blackfriars Road, over Waterloo Bridge. From these breeders other addresses can be obtained, and stocks examined." We may add, also, that very superior specimens of the lop-eared rabbits may be obtained, in this country, of F. Rotch, Esq., and R. H. Van Rensselaer, of Morris (formerly Butternuts), Otsego County, New York.

PROPERTIES REQUIRED FOR PRIZES.

In competing for prizes in England, there are seven properties required:—First. Length of ears—the longer, the better. Second. The width of ears. Third. Carriage of the ears—i. e., the way they fall. They ought to be nearly perpendicular in their fall—that is, so as to drop close to the outer corner of the eye. Fourth. The size and form of the eye—the larger and fuller, the better. Fifth. Color of the fur. These are blue and white, yellow and white, gray and white tortoise-shell, black and white, gray, black, blue, and white, with red eyes. Sixth. Shape. Of the general beauty of form, any common observer can judge. High forehead and broad poll are required for first-class animals. Seventh. Weight. At a little over seven months, the heaviest are from ten to twelve pounds. They are not permitted to compete for prizes beyond eight months old.

A correspondent of the *Cottage Gardener* states himself to be a rabbit-fancier of thirty years' standing, and that he bred the longest-eared rabbit ever known. He has her (for it was a doe) preserved in a glass case. Her ears, from tip to tip, measured twenty-two inches, and each ear in width was five inches and three-eighths. Her weight was eighteen pounds.

FEEDING AND KILLING FOR THE TABLE.

THE flavor of tame rabbits is improved by feeding them, a few days before they are killed, on aromatic plants, of which the list is numerous. Some people also fill the belly of the rabbit, after it is killed and drawn, with a wisp of thyme, marjoram, and sage. The usual mode of killing tame rabbits, by giving them a blow behind the ear, is faulty, and liable to the objection that a large quantity of blood coagulates about the place which is struck. It is better to kill them exactly like fowls, by cutting the jugular artery, and then to hang them up by the hind legs. In that position the blood drains away, and the flesh is rendered beautifully white. The skins, however, suffer, and sell for less if they are besmeared with blood. The cook's perquisite is thus diminished; and, in rabbit-keeping on a large scale, the reduction of price would be of serious importance.

CASTRATION.

THE contempt with which such small cattle as rabbits are usually regarded by practical people, is the cause why they are but rarely subjected to the operation of castration, which, in their case, is performed with greater ease, and even with more satisfactory results, than on oxen, sheep, and pigs. We have eaten caponized rabbits; and they were far superior, in size, flavor, and fatness, to what they would have been if suffered to remain in their natural state. We would advise every rabbit-keeper to castrate, at the age of three or four months, every young buck which he does not intend to dispose of or retain for breeding purposes. Besides the rapid increase in size, a great advantage gained is the conversion of a mischievous into an inoffensive animal. Instead of being often a dangerous enemy to the does, to the young ones, and to the other bucks (for the males, if not so treated, will engage in deadly combats when they meet), it may then be suffered to associate indiscriminately with the others, without fear or apprehension.

The mode of castrating rabbits is very simple. It is performed by seizing with the thumb and the two first fingers of the left hand one of the testicles, which the animal will endeavor to draw up internally. When the operator has succeeded in grasping it, he divides the skin

longitudinally with a sharp knife, presses outwards the
oval body which he has seized, draws it out, and throws
it away. After repeating the performance on the other
side, he anoints the wounds with a little fresh hog's lard,
or he closes them by a stitch with a needle and thread—
or perhaps he leaves the cure to nature. When the operation is skilfully performed, the healing process is rapidly
completed; and it not only disposes the animal to carry
a great deal more flesh and fat, but the skin also is con-
siderably increased in value.

DISEASES.

THEIR PREVENTION AND CURE.

" AMONGST rabbits, as with poultry, diseases are more
easily prevented than cured. We have seen advertised
in the newspapers specific medicines for ailing rabbits.
'Roup and Condition Pills,' and 'The Poultry Restora-
tive—a certain Cure for all Diseases,' may probably be
useful tonics in the case of fowls; but with the delicate
species of quadruped which is the subject of the present
treatise, negligence and mismanagement are so fearfully
punished, that it strongly behoves the amateur to take
care that his arrangements and mode of feeding be such
as to give him the least amount possible of disease to
deal with. The loss of whole litters at once, or even a
general mortality amongst his entire stock, will often be the
consequence of carelessness and want of judgment. Many
and many a small farmer and market gardener has made

attempts to keep rabbits, and has soon given them up again, in utter disgust at the complete want of success which has attended his efforts. A few plain hints might have saved him the disappointment, and have enabled him to conduct his experiment with a more satisfactory and profitable result. On this account, we think it right to give a few short paragraphs on rabbit disease a place in our practical essay."

Bedding.—"Thus, the quality of the litter given to domestic rabbits is a very essential point in rearing them successfully. The bad state of that is the cause of many diseases to which they are liable. The straw used for this purpose ought to be thoroughly dry, and frequently renewed. Every three weeks, the entire mass of their litter should be changed, especial care being taken to have it done a fortnight before the doe kindles, and a fortnight after the birth of the little ones. It is a good plan, during the interval, to cover the old litter with a sprinkling of fresh straw from time to time."

Injudicious disturbance, also, will sometimes have as fatal an effect as a severe epidemic. We have seen that it is absolutely necessary not to be too much in a hurry to look at the young ones, for at least a week after their birth. It should also be remembered that the rabbit is naturally an animal of nocturnal, or we ought rather to say crepuscular, that is, *twilight* habits. It is therefore an error to believe that it is requisite to give them a substantial meal at noon; on the contrary, nature and observation indicate that they ought to be left in quiet at that hour, when they are almost always in a state of repose, especially during summer. The best feeding-times are, very early indeed in the morning, and about sunset in the evening. They usually eat with the greatest appetite during the night."

Quiet.—However, one little act of disturbance may be ventured upon with due precaution. A few days after the birth of the rabbits, it will be advisable to ascertain whether their mother has deposited them in a dry spot; for if their nest is at all damp, they will infallibly perish. In such a case, the nest must be cautiously moved, in a lump, and shifted to the driest corner of the hutch. Experience has proved that this operation, if judiciously executed, caused no injury whatever to the young, and also gave no offence to the mother; but, after all, the expedient must be used with caution. The inconvenience which compels the rabbit-keeper to have recourse to it ought to be avoided by cleansing the hutches at regular periods, so that there shall be no necessity to intrude upon the privacy of the doe's nursery at the time when she is likely to be of a susceptible and jealous disposition. For this purpose, it is requisite to note accurately the date of the doe's visits to the buck, in order to be able to change the litter in good time, and also to remove a first set of young ones, when there is a prospect of their soon being followed by a second.

Ophthalmia.—"Young are subject to a disease of the eyes, which is apt to attack them towards the end of their suckling, and which puts an end to them in a very short time. The disease is unknown to those who are scrupulous about the cleanliness and drainage of their hutches. It appears to be occasioned by the putrid exhalations from filth and urine in a decomposing state. In short, it is nei-

4*

ther more nor less than ophthalmia, brought on by the caustic nature of ammonial vapor. When the malady is discovered in time, the young rabbits may sometimes be saved by transferring them into another hutch that is perfectly clean, and well furnished with plenty of fresh straw."

The Rot and Pot-Belly.—"The great cause of the shortness of rabbits' lives in domesticity is their liability to *the rot*, or liver-disease, produced by their being supplied with too much green food. Dry food, in short, is the grand thing to insure success in rabbit-keeping. That peculiar quality of diet is so absolutely necessary to the animals' well-being, that 'DRY FOOD,' in capital letters, ought to be painted within sight of every rabbit menagerie, whatever may be its form, size, or importance. Even the wild races, in wet seasons, are found lying about dead, as if their warren had been stricken with pestilence. The *rot* is as fatal to rabbits as to sheep. Therefore a very necessary precaution, which cannot be too strictly insisted on, is to avoid giving tame rabbits too great a quantity of green and succulent herbage, which not only causes numerous deaths from indigestion, but what is worse, is apt to bring on another disease, only of too common occurrence, which is occasioned by the accumulation of an excessive quantity of water in the abdomen and bladder, and which usually proves fatal. The patient, in fact, becomes dropsical; and even if apparently cured for a time, is so apt to suffer a relapse, that the wisest way is to part with the animal. Rabbits so diseased are said to be '*pot-bellied;*' and when they get to an advanced stage of the complaint, doctoring is of but little use, and generally of none at all. Common rabbits, in such case, are hardly worth the trouble of nursing. For fancy kinds of greater value, the attempt may be made; but we much more strongly urge the observance of preventive than of remedial measures.

"The patients should be immediately put upon a drier diet. Pamper them with split peas, barley-meal, malt-combs, and oatmeal. Oak leaves, and the shoots of the tree, as food, are excellent. They should have hay, sound corn, and aromatic plants, such as thyme, sage, marjoram, &c. In fact, all rabbit-masters who have a garden, will do well to cultivate an extra-sized bed of sweet herbs, as the best apothecary's shop which they can have recourse to in time of need. The whole family of umbelliferous plants appear to be both grateful and medicinal to the rabbit tribe; even hemlock and fool's parsley, poisonous plants to many other animals, are welcome as occasional dainties to them; hog-weed, or the wild perennial parsnip, has been recommended by Cobbett, with his usual force of natural eloquence. Garden parsnips and carrots are excellent, both for their tops and roots; likewise fennel, parsley, and chervil.

"If the sick quadrupeds are kept to a regimen that is absolutely dry, a *little* may now and then be given them; at all other times, it is absolutely a forbidden thing. But wetted herbage, we insist, even if only moistened with dew, is poison to rabbits. The best mode of avoiding danger is to cut their food the day before, and spread it out, in the sunshine or under shelter, to dry and wither. On the other hand, it ought not to be cut several days beforehand; for if thrown into a heap, and so left to heat,

it is likely to prove equally injurious. Of course, all diseased individuals should be carefully separated from those
that are in health.

" The same prudential sanitary measure is imperative
when rabbits are attacked by a sort of consumption, or
'rot,' which reduces them to the extreme of leanness, and
they become covered with a contagious scabbiness, which
is extremely difficult to cure. This disease, which attacks
them when young, checks their growth, takes away their
appetite, and at last causes them to die in violent convul-
sions. If it is not arrested in time, it may soon spread
throughout the whole of the stud. It is usually attributed
to damp and superabundant moisture in various forms,
which seem to be mortal enemies of the rabbit. As pot-
belly, or dropsy, is caused by a too succulent vegetable
diet, so 'rot' is brought on by eating putrid greens, or
even those that are in the 'heated' state of incipient fer-
mentation. It is believed that the repeated indulgence in
this kind of unnatural and unwholesome food produces
the purulent pustules with which the unfortunate animal's
liver is sometimes entirely covered, as well as engender-
ing, we know not how, the parasitic creatures called
flukes, or hydatids, that are found in the substance of the
diseased liver. The remedies, with the addition of salt,
are nearly the same both for 'pot-belly' and 'rot;' indeed, it is not very easy to distinguish them till after a
somewhat advanced period. Flour of sulphur, sprinkled
on the skin, has been recommended in case of mange or
scab. The wisest way, however, is to prevent the further
spreading of the contagious form of disease, by sacrificing
at once the animal that is attacked by it."

Red Water.—Besides the former, there are a few maladies which only make their appearance in badly-attended and mismanaged studs, or during unusually fatal seasons; such as *red water*, produced by inflammation of the kidneys and a highly febrile state·of the animal. High-colored urine is then voided, in its worst stage mingled with blood. Bad food, acrid and poisonous vegetables, or sudden chills, may either of them be the immediate cause of the complaint. The remedy will be, mild mucilaginous food, such as endive, dandelion, sow-thistle, lettuce (but not after it sends up its seed-stalk), with cooked potatoes and bran, besides a warm and cleanly lodging.

The Snuffles.—"This is occasioned by catching a violent cold in the head, and may degenerate into bronchitis and inflammation of the lungs. Comfortable shelter, and protection from all draughts and wet, is the cure which common sense prescribes."

Diarrhœa, or undue looseness of the bowels, is the result of eating too great a quantity of wet and acrid rubbish. Dry food must be again the prescription; add to it bread-crusts and the skins of baked potatoes. To avoid the evil, it should be particularly borne in mind that all changes of diet with a confined animal, especially from a drier to a moister—and in spring and autumn—should be *gradually* made. No stock of any kind, not even of transitions of regimen, ought ever to be given to the system of so nervous a creature as the rabbit is.

Rare Cases.—"Human pathology and surgery has its chapter exclusively devoted to *rare cases;* the same thing occurs with fowls and with rabbits. One of these is furnished by a correspondent of the *Cottage Gardener:*—

'On examining a rabbit of the lop-eared breed to-day, I found one ear completely filled with a hard matter resembling scurf. On touching the ear, the rabbit screamed out. I then took as much of the hard stuff off as I could, and bathed with warm water; after that, I greased the ear well. I took two pieces as large as a man's finger from the ear, which seemed to reach quite to the farthest extremity.' Many others, no doubt, might be added; but they are more valuable as curious facts, than as being of any great practical utility."—DELAMER.

AMERICAN GRAY RABBIT.

AMERICAN GRAY RABBIT.

In the Natural History of the State of New York, by Dr. De Kay, we find a full description and figure of the native wild rabbit of this country, which we have copied from that work.

This common and well-known species in the United States has been, until very recently, confounded with others. The following, by Schreber, which seems to have been overlooked by modern writers, applies remarkably well to our rabbit. Although misled by the accounts of previous naturalists, he appears to have confounded its history with the former species:—Cheeks full of thick hair. Ears thin externally, with few hairs, naked within, and when bent forward, do not reach the nose; when bent backward, they reach the shoulder-blades. Eyes large and black, with four to five bristles above them. Whiskers mostly black; some are white; the longest appears to reach beyond the head. Color in summer:—ears brownish, with a very narrow black border on the outer margin, of the same breadth of the tips, or becomes effaced; brown cheeks, back, and sides; fore and hind legs light brown externally, mixed with black; all around the breech white. Feet full of short hair, of a light brown, unmixed with black, changing towards the inside to a gray white. Upper part of the tail like that of the back (perhaps mixed with black, as Pennant describes it black); beneath, white. Throat white; lower part of the neck bright brown, mixed with white; chest and belly, inside of fore and hind legs, white color in winter, when it does not change, white.

Its food consists of bark, grass, wild berries, &c.; and in cultivated districts, it is said to enter gardens and destroy vegetables. Unlike its congeners, it does not confine itself to the woods, but is frequently found in open fields, or where there is a slight copse or underbrush. It does not burrow, like its closely allied species, the European rabbit, but makes its form, which is a slight depression in the ground, sheltered by some low shrub. It frequently resorts to a stone wall, or a heap of stones, or hollow tree, and sometimes to the burrow of some other animal. Its habits are nocturnal; and they may often be seen in the morning, or early part of the forenoon, although in retired situations they have been seen at all times of the day. Its flesh, though black and dry, is well flavored, although in this respect it varies with the quality of its previous food. It breeds in this State, as I have been informed, three times in the season, producing from four to six at a birth. It is the smallest of the species found in this State, and so much resembles in its form the European rabbit, that the same popular name has been applied to it, although differing in color and some of its habits. This, however, is of no consequence, for the name of American Gray Rabbit is sufficiently distinctive.

It has a wide geographical range. It is found from New Hampshire to Florida, but its Western limits are not yet established.

THE NORTHERN VARYING HARE.

The author has noticed this rabbit on Staten Island, on Becroft's Mountain, east of the city of Hudson, on the pine plains west of Albany, and also on the high-lands and plains of Saratoga.

THE NORTHERN VARYING HARE.

"ALL the species of the genus Lepus hitherto discovered in America," remarks the editor of the Cabinet of Natural History, "have the habits of the Hare, though they are generally called Rabbits." We will at present confine our observations to the subject of our illustration, which has given rise to some diversity of opinion among naturalists, though it has long been known to hunters and fur-traders as different from the common species.

As was the case with almost all the American animals resembling those of the old continent, early naturalists considered it as identical with the analogous European species. The first description given of it in any detail is by Hearne. "The *varying* hares are numerous, and extend as far as latitude 72° N., and probably farther. They delight most in rocky and stony places, near the borders of woods, though many of them brave the coldest winters on entirely barren ground. In summer, they are nearly of the color of the English wild rabbit, but in winter assume a most delicate white all over, except the tips of the ears, which are black. They are, when full grown and in good condition, very large, many of them weighing fourteen or fifteen pounds."

The dimensions of this species, on the authority of

Bachman, vary from seventeen to twenty-five inches. It
is remarkable how two observers have so widely differed
in their accounts of the dimensions of the same specimens.
Bonaparte gives the total length at thirty-one inches;
Harlan's measurement of the same specimen makes it but
sixteen inches.   These statements may be reconciled,
when we recollect that the latter measured from the specimen when recent, and probably represented the distance
from the nose to the extremity of the hind legs.

The American Varying Hare appears to inhabit a great
portion of North America, as it has been found in Vir-
ginia, and as far North as 55°.   It appears generally to
frequent plains and low grounds, where it lives like the
common hare, never burrowing, but does not resort to the
thick woods.   The *variabilis* of Europe, on the contrary,
is described as always inhabiting the highest mountains,
and never descending into the plains, except when forced
to seek food, when the mountains are covered with snow.
The American Hare is remarkably swift, never taking
shelter when pursued, and is capable of taking astonishing
leaps: Captain Lewis measured some of these, and found
their length from eighteen to twenty-one feet.   Warden,
however, states that this species, when pursued, will re-
treat into hollow trees.

They, like all the hares, are very prolific, the female
having several litters a year, of five or six leverets at a
litter.

The voice of these animals is seldom or never heard,
except when they are irritated or wounded, when they
utter a loud, piercing cry, bearing some resemblance to
that of a child in pain.   We have been informed by an

eye-witness, that he saw an European buck rabbit attack a cat, and rip open its bowels by a single stroke of its hind claws.

One of the most remarkable peculiarities of this genus is the difference of habits between some of the species, closely allied as they are in their physical appearance. Thus, the rabbit and the hare, although furnished with analogous organs, and inhabiting in many instances the same countries, manifest the greatest aversion for each other—a hatred which M. F. Cuvier asserts nothing can obliterate; for, however nearly they assimilated in form or character, they never associate; and, when they meet, a combat generally ensues, which often terminates fatally to one of the parties.

One striking point of dissimilarity between the hare and rabbit is, that whilst the hare merely forms a shallow hollow in the earth for her form or nest, the rabbit excavates deep and tortuous burrows.

If taken young, the hare may be tamed and domesticated, and has been nursed by a cat. Sonnini, the naturalist, and Cowper, the poet, had hares in a complete state of domestication. Although exceedingly timid and watchful, the hare is capable of being domesticated, and even taught a variety of tricks.

One was exhibited in London, some time since, which could play on the tamborine, discharge a pistol, and perform a variety of feats of as strange a character for an animal of so fearful disposition.

COOKING RABBITS.

HAVING in the foregoing pages given all the information we possess in regard to the selecting, breeding, and general management of the rabbit, we will now proceed to give a few recipes for cooking the same.

Boiled Rabbit, smothered with Onion Sauce.—They must be skewered and trussed, so as to come to table in a crouching posture. Dust it with flour, as you would a boiled chicken, to make it come out the whiter. Tie it in a cloth; if young, put it into boiling-hot water; if old, into cold water. The time of boiling must be entirely regulated by the apparent age and tenderness of the rabbit. N. B.—Tomato instead of onion sauce is a much approved variation of this dish.

While the rabbit is boiling, prepare your onion sauce thus:—Peel your onions, halve and quarter them, put them on in a sauce-pan in cold water, boil till perfectly soft, strain them from the water, and then braid them through a colander. To the pulp thus made add a lump of butter and some thick cream, with a little pepper and salt. Then make it just boil up, being careful that it does not burn, and pour it over the rabbit as it lies on its dish. Serve at the same time a piece of boiled white bacon to eat with it, and a tureen of melted butter.

Roast Rabbit.—*A genuine Warren Recipe.*—Make a force-meat of bread-crumbs, minced beef-suet, lemon-peel, nutmeg, pepper and salt, and a little lemon-thyme, if sweet herbs are approved. Beat up two eggs, and mix with them, the whole into paste. Put this force-meat inside the rabbit, and sew it up, and skewer it into the proper form. Rub the outside of the rabbit over with butter, flour it a little, and stick on very thin slices of bacon by means of small skewers of iron wire. A French cook would lard them with a larding-needle. These slices of bacon will roast up till they are become quite crisp and dry ; the fat which oozes from them will keep the rabbit moist and juicy. Still, it ought to be well basted while roasting. Make a gravy with a small piece of beef (or the livers of rabbits, if they are not roasted inside), a whole onion put in without peeling it, some whole pepper-corns, a blade of mace, and a clove or two, with a small crust of bread toasted very dry and brown, but not burnt. When the gravy is boiled enough, strain it, and a little catsup and flour well braided together. Make the gravy *just boil up* (not for a minute or two), before serving with the roast rabbit, in a separate tureen by itself. Some add a glass of port wine to the gravy.

Stewed Rabbit.—Cut the rabbits into joints. Half fry them into butter, and lay them into a stew-pan. Fry some sliced onions, and put them over the rabbit in the stew-pan, with a little powdered mace, pepper, and salt. Pour sufficient water over them to cover them, allowing for the waste by evaporation during cooking. The stew must be done very slowly, only being allowed just to simmer. It

5

will take two hours to do it properly; when enough, take out each piece of rabbit and lay it on the dish on which it is to be served; with the gravy which remains in the stew-pan mix a pickled walnut finely and smoothly braided, with a good tablespoonful of catsup and a dust of flour. Set it over the fire, and pour it over your rabbit directly that it shows symptoms of boiling up.

Rabbit Pie.—Cut the rabbits into joints, and simply stew them with water, pepper, salt, and pounded mace, till they are half done. Proceed then as for pigeon pie, putting veal or pork, or both, instead of the beef. Cover with paste, and bake till enough.

To Curry Rabbits.—Take a young rabbit or two, skin and cut them into conveniently-sized pieces to serve, put them into a frying-pan with some butter, and fry them of a nice light brown color; then place them at the bottom of your stew-pan.

Slice and fry six or eight large onions; place them over the rabbit in the stew-pan. Then mix four tablespoonsful of best curry-powder and some good stock gravy (which is a great point in insuring success), with salt, Cayenne pepper, nutmeg, three or four slices of lemon with the peel on, a small quantity of chopped pickles of all kinds that are at hand, and a glass of sherry.

Boil well, and pour it over the rabbit and onions in the stew-pan; let all simmer together for three hours; serve it up in a dish encircled with rice that has been boiled in the following manner: Put the rice in cold water, and when it boils let it boil *exactly sixteen minutes* afterwards. The *seventeenth* minute would spoil it utterly. It is as with the charmed bullets of Zamial, "The six(-teenth) shall achieve, the seven(-teenth) deceive."

FRENCH WAYS OF COOKING RABBITS.

Marinade of Rabbit.—The French have the habit of steeping or pickling many viands, especially white meats and fresh-water fish, in what they call *marinade*, or pickle, of various compositions.

If you are going to make use of a tame rabbit, hulk it as soon as it is killed, and stuff the inside with thyme, bay-leaves, sage, basil, pepper, and salt. Roast it till it is half done, and let it get cold. Cut it into joints, and put them into a *marinade* composed of white wine (or cider), lemon-juice, and parsley, shallots, thyme, bay-leaves, and a clove of garlic, all chopped up fine together. After they have soaked an hour, dip them in butter, and fry them in oil or butter which is not too hot. Fry them to a bright clear brown, and serve them dry, garnished with fried parsley.

Gibbelotte is the name of a particular mode of stew or fricassee, in which various meats and poultry may be served. Gibbelotte of rabbit (which is the original *gibelotte*) is thus made: Cut a rabbit into joints. Put a lump of butter into a stew-pan, and some lean bacon cut into slices. When they are browned take them out, and put your rabbit in. As soon as it has had a toss or two, add a spoon-

ful of flour, a glass of white wine, and a glass of good
broth, a little pepper and nutmeg, a dozen small onions, a
few button mushrooms, or instead of them a dessert spoon-
ful of mushroom catsup, and a bunch of sweet herbs.
When the rabbit is done enough, take the fat off the
gravy; thicken it if required, so that it be neither too
thick nor too thin; pour it over the rabbit, and serve
garnished, either with pieces of toast or of fried bread
round the dish.

It is not an uncommon practice with French cooks *to
add an eel or two cut into short pieces,* when this and similar
dishes are half cooked, and then to serve the whole together.

Civet is the French name appropriated to a dish of stewed
hare; but rabbits are commonly dressed in the same way,
when hares are out of season.

Civet of Rabbit is made by cutting it into joints, putting
it into a stew-pan, and giving it two or three turns on the
fire. Then add a dusting of flour, a liberal allowance of
red-wine, salt, pepper, and a few slices of bacon. Throw
in some small onions that have been fried whole in butter,
with a bouquet of sweet herbs. Make it boil up and skim
off the fat. As soon as it is done enough, take away the
bouquet, and serve hot. N. B.—But a small quantity of
the gravy should come to table.

Rabbit Paté.—A very useful standing dish may be made
of any size, the larger the better.

Have ready your rabbits; cut them up into joints; have,
also, an earthen or stoneware *paté*-dish with a close-fitting

cover. This kind of *paté* is made without any crust. At the bottom of the dish lay slices of bacon, and over that a layer of minced meat, of any kind you happen to have at hand, mixed with chopped parsley, chives, a large clove of garlic, mushrooms, and pepper. Upon this bed lay the whole of your rabbits, as closely as you can pack the pieces, and then the remainder of your mince-meat, and some more slices of bacon to cover the whole. Shake it well together. Throw in a glass or two of white wine, put the cover on the dish, and set it in the oven till it is done enough. It must not be touched to be eaten until it is cold.

En papillottes, or *in curl-papers*, is a favorite French way of serving small portions of meat, such as joints of poultry and game, chops, cutlets, &c.

For rabbits in curl-papers, cut them into quarters if they are very young, and into joints if they are full-grown; *marinade*, or pickle them, several hours in a mixture of oil, salt, pepper, catsup, and chopped parsley and chives, well mingled together. Have ready some oiled or buttered white writing paper, prepared exactly as for cutlets *en papillotes;* do up each piece of rabbit with a little of the seasoning and a thin slice of bacon enclosed in the paper; grill them on a gridiron over a very slow fire, and when they are thoroughly done serve them smoking hot in the paper, just as they are.

END.

BOOKS FOR THE COUNTRY,

PUBLISHED BY

C. M. SAXTON,

152 FULTON STREET, NEW YORK,

SUITABLE FOR

SCHOOL, TOWN, AGRICULTURAL AND PRIVATE LIBRARIES.

The American Cattle Doctor;

Containing the necessary information for preserving the health and curing the diseases of Oxen, Cows, Sheep and Swine, with a great variety of original receipts, and valuable information in reference to Farm and Dairy management, whereby every man can be his own Cattle Doctor The principles taught in this work are, that all medication shall be subservient to nature—that all medicines must be sanative in their operation, and administered with a view of aiding the vital powers, instead of depressing as heretofore, with the lancet by poison By G. H Dodd, M.D, Veterinary Practitioner. Price $1.

The Field Book of Manures;

Or American Muck Book , treating of the Nature, Properties. Sources, History, and Operations of all the principal Fertilizers and Manures in Common Use, with Specific Directions for their Preservation, and Application to the Soil and to Crops ; drawn from Authentic Sources, Actual Experience, and Personal Observation, as combined with the leading Principles of Practical and Scientific Agriculture By D Jay Brown. $1.25.

Sheep Husbandry;

With an account of the different breeds, and general directions in regard to Sum mer and Winter management, breeding, and the treatment of diseases, with portraits and other engravings By Henry S Randall Price $1 25

Blake's Farmer at Home.

A Family Text Book for the Country ; being a Cyclopædia of Agricultural Imple- ments and Productions, and of the more Important Topics in Domestic Economy, Science and Literature , adapted to Rural Life By Rev John L. Blake, D D $1 25

The Progressive Farmer.

A Scientific Treatise on Agricultural Chemistry, the Geology of Agriculture, on Plants and Animals, Manures and Soils applied to Practical Agriculture by J A Nash Price 50 cts

Allen on the Culture of the Grape.

A Practical Treatise on the Culture and Treatment of the Grape Vine, embracing its history, with directions for its treatment in the United States of America, in the open air and under glass structures, with and without artificial heat By J Fisk Allen Price $1

Mysteries of Bee-keeping Explained;

Being a Complete Analysis of the whole subject, consisting of the Natural History of Bees, Directions for Obtaining the greatest amount of Pure Surplus Honey with the least possible expense , Remedies for Losses given, and the Science of Luck , fully illustrated ; the result of more than twenty years' experience in extensive Aviaries By M Quinby. Price $1

The Shepherd's Own Book;

With an Account of the different Breeds and Management, and Diseases of Sheep; and General Directions in regard to Summer and Winter Management, Breeding, and the Treatment of Diseases, with Illustrative Engravings, by Youatt & Ran dall, embracing Skinner's Notes on the Breed and Management of Sheep in the United States, and on the Culture of Fine Wool. Price $2

Canfield on Sheep.

The Breeds, Management, Structure and Diseases of the Sheep, with Illustrative Engravings, and an Appendix, containing List of Medicines used in the Treatment of Diseases, Plans of Stalls Gates, Barn, Sheds, &c &c. Price $1.

Johnston's Chemistry and Geology.

Elements of Agricultural Chemistry and Geology, with a Complete Analytical and Alphabetical Index. By Simon Brown, Esq, Editor of the New England Farmer. Price $1 25

Practical Agriculture;

Being a Treatise on the General Relations which Science bears to Agriculture Delivered before the New York State Agricultural Society; with Notes and Ex planations by an American Farmer. Cloth. 75 cts., paper 50 cts

Johnston's Agricultural Chemistry.

Lectures on the Application of Chemistry and Geology to Agriculture. New edition, with an Appendix $1.25

Smith's Landscape Gardening, Parks & Pleasure Grounds;

With Practical Notes on Country Residences, Villas, Public Parks and Gardens. By Charles H J. Smith, Landscape Gardener and Garden Architect, &c., with Notes and Additions by Lewis F Allen, author of "Rural Architecture," &c.

The author, while engaged in his profession for the last eighteen years, has often been requested to recommend a book which might enable persons to acquire some general knowledge of the principles of Landscape Gardening.

The object of the present work is to preserve a plain and direct method of statement, to be intelligible to all who have had an ordinary education, and to give directions which, it is hoped, will be found to be practical by those who have an adequate knowledge of country affairs Price $1 25

Guide to the Orchard and Fruit Garden;

Or an Account of the most valuable Fruits Cultivated in Great Britain By George Lindley, with additions of all the most valuable Fruits Cultivated in America, with Directions for their Cultivation, Budding, Grafting and Propagation; Pruning and Training of Standards, Open Dwarf and Espalier Fruit Trees, adapted to the Climate of the United States of America A new edition, with an Appendix, describing many American Fruits not mentioned in the former edition. Price $ 125.

The American Fruit Culturist;

Containing Directions for the Propagation and Culture of Fruit Trees in the Nursery, Orchard and Garden, with Descriptions of the principal American and Foreign varieties Cultivated in the United States By John J. Thomas Illustrated with three hundred accurate figures. Price $1.25

American Poultry Yard.

The American Poultry Yard; comprising the Origin, History and Description of the different Breeds of Domestic Poultry, with complete directions for their Breeding, Crossing, Rearing, Fattening and Preparation for Market; including specific directions for Caponizing Fowls, and for the Treatment of the Principal Diseases to which they are subject drawn from authentic sources and personal observation Illustrated with numerous engravings. By D. J. Browne Cloth $1; paper, 75 cts

Youatt and Martin on Cattle;

Being a Treatise on their Breeds, Management and Diseases, comprising a full History of the Various Races; their Origin, Breeding and Merits; their capacity for Beef and Milk By W Youatt and W C. L. Martin The whole forming a complete Guide for the Farmer, the Amateur, and the Veterinary Surgeon, with 100 illustrations Edited by Ambrose Stevens $1.25

Youatt on the Horse.

Youatt on the Structure and Diseases of the Horse, with their Remedies Also, Practical Rules for Buyers, Breeders, Smiths, &c. Edited by W. C. Spooner, M R C V S With an account of the Breeds in the United States, by Henry S Randall $1.25

Youatt and Martin on the Hog.

A Treatise on the Breeds, Management and Medical Treatment of Swine, with directions for Salting Pork and Curing Bacon and Hams. By Wm. Youatt, R. S. Illustrated with engravings drawn from life $1 00.

Youatt on Sheep;

Their Breed, Management and Diseases, with illustrative engravings; to which are added Remarks on the Breeds and Management of Sheep in the United States, and on the Culture of Fine Wool in Silesia By William Youatt 75 cts

American Architect.

The American Architect, comprising Original Designs of cheap Country and Village Residences, with Details, Specifications, Plans and Directions, and an estimate of the Cost of each Design By John W. Ritch, Architect First and Second Series, quarto, bound in one vol, half roan, $6

Domestic Medicine.

Gunn's Domestic Medicine, or Poor Man's Friend in the Hours of Affliction, Pain and Sickness Raymond's new revised edition, improved and enlarged by John C Gunn, 8vo Sheep, $3

Family Kitchen Gardener;

Containing Plain and Accurate Descriptions of all the different Species and Varieties of Culinary Vegetables, with their Botanical, English, French and German names, alphabetically arranged, and the best mode of cultivating them in the garden, or under glass, also, Descriptions and Character of the most Select Fruits; their Management, Propagation, &c By Robert Buist, author of the American Flower Garden Directory, &c Cloth, 75 cts., paper, 50 cts

Hoare on the Grape Vine.

A Practical Treatise on the Cultivation of the Grape Vine on Open Walls, with a Descriptive Account of an improved method of Planting and Managing the Roots of Grape Vines By Clement Hoare With an Appendix on the Cultivation of the same in the United States. 50 cts.

Stephens' Book of the Farm;

A Complete Guide to the Farmer, Steward, Plowman, Cattleman, Shepherd, Field Worker and Dairy Maid By Henry Stephens With Four Hundred and Fifty Illustrations, to which are added Explanatory Notes, Remarks, &c, by J. S Skinner Really one of the best books for a Farmer to possess. Cloth, $4. leather, $4.50.

The Diseases of Domestic Animals;

Being a History and Description of the Horse, Mule, Cattle, Sheep, Swine, Poultry and Farm Dogs, with Directions for their Management, Breeding, Crossing, Rearing, Feeding and Preparation for a profitable Market, also, their Diseases and Remedies, together with full Directions for the Management of the Dairy, and the Comparative Economy and Advantages of Working Animals, the Horse, Mule, Oxen, &c By R L Allen Cloth, 75 cts, paper, 50 cts

American Bee-keeper's Manual ;

Being a Practical Treatise on the History and Domestic Economy of the Honey Bee, embracing a full illustration of the whole subject, with the most approved methods of managing this Insect, through every branch of its Culture, the result of many years experience Illustrated with many engravings. By T. B. Miner. Cloth, $1.

American Bird Fancier,

Considered with reference to the Breeding, Rearing, Feeding, Management, &c of Cage and House Birds. Illustrated with engravings. By D J. Browne. Cloth, 50 cts.

The American Farm Book.

The American Farm Book ; or, a Compend of American Agriculture, being a Practical Treatise on Soils, Manures, Draining, Irrigation, Grasses, Grain, Roots, Fruits, Cotton, Tobacco, Sugar Cane, Rice, and every Staple Product of the United States, with the best methods of planting, cultivating and preparation for market. Illustrated by more than 100 engravings. By R. L. Allen. Cloth, $1 , paper, 75 cents

Southern Agriculture ;

Comprising Essays on the Cultivation of Corn, Hemp, Tobacco, Wheat, &c. $1

The Cottage and Farm Bee-keeper ;

A Practical Work, by a Country Curate 50 cts

A Book for Every Boy in the Country.

Elements of Agriculture. Translated from the French, and adapted to general use, by F G Skinner. 25 cts

Allen's Rural Architecture ;

Comprising Farm Houses, Cottages, Carriage Houses, Sheep and Dove Cotes, Piggeries, Barns, &c &c. By Lewis F. Allen $1.25.

The Rose ;

Being a Practical Treatise on the Propagation, Cultivation and Management of the Rose in all Seasons ; with a List of Choice and Approved Varieties, adapted to the Climate of the United States, to which is added Full Directions for the Treatment of the Dahlia Illustrated by engravings. Cloth, 50 cts

The American Agriculturist ;

Being a Collection of Original Articles on the Various Subjects connected with the Farm, in ten vols 8vo, containing nearly four thousand pages $10.

The Complete Farmer and American Gardener,

Rural Economist, and New American Gardener, containing a Compendious Epitome of the most Important Branches of Agricultural and Rural Economy ; with Practical Directions on the Cultivation of Fruits and Vegetables, including Landscape and Ornamental Gardening By Thomas G Fessenden. 2 vols in one. $1.25

Experimental Researches on the Food of Animals,

The Fattening of Cattle, and Remarks on the Food of Man. By Robert Dundas Thompson, M D. 75 cts

The American Florist's Guide ;

Comprising the American Rose Culturist and Every Lady her own Flower Gardener. Half cloth, 75 cts

Saxton's Rural Hand Books,

First and Second Series Bound in 2 vols. $2 50 Embracing Twelve Complete Treatises in the different departments of Agriculture, being one of the most valuable Books yet published

SAXTON'S
HAND BOOKS OF RURAL AND DOMESTIC ECONOMY
All Arranged and Adapted to the Use of American Farmers.

Price 25 Cents each

Hogs;

Their Origin and Varieties; Management, with a View to Profit, and Tres'ment under Disease, also, Plain Directions relative to the most approved modes of preserving their flesh. By H. D Richardson, author of "The Hive and the Honey Bee," &c &c With illustrations—19mo

The Hive and Honey Bee,

With plain directions for obtaining a considerable Annual Income from this branch of Rural Economy, also an Account of the Diseases of Bees, and their Remedies, and Remarks as to their Enemies, and the best mode of protecting the Hives from their attacks. By H D Richardson With Illustrations

Domestic Fowls;

Their Natural History, Breeding, Rearing and General Management By H D Richardson, author of "The Natural History of the Fossil Deer," &c With Illustrations

The Horse;

Their Origin and Varieties, with Plain Directions as to the Breeding, Rearing and General Management, with Instructions as to the Treatment of Disease. Handsomely Illustrated—12mo By H D Richardson

The Rose;

The American Rose Culturist, being a Practical Treatise on the Propagation, Cultivation and Management in all Seasons, &c With full directions for the Treatment of the Dahlia

The Pests of the Farm;

With Instructions for their Extirpation, being a Manual of Plain Directions for the certain Destruction of every description of Vermin With numerous Illustrations on Wood.

An Essay on Manures;

Submitted to the Trustees of the Massachusetts Society for Promoting Agriculture, for their Premium. By Samuel H Dana

The American Bird Fancier;

Considered with reference to the Breeding, Rearing, Feeding, Management and Peculiarities of Cage and House Birds. Illustrated with Engravings. By D Jay Browne

Chemistry Made Easy,

For the Use of Farmers By J Topham

Elements of Agriculture;

Translated from the French, and Adapted to the use of American Farmers. By F. G. Skinner.

The American Kitchen Gardener;

Containing Directions for the Cultivation of Vegetables and Garden Fruits. By T. G. Fessenden.

The Bee Keeper's Chart;

Being a brief practical Treatise on the Instinct, Habits and Management of the Honey Bee, in all its various Branches, tho result of many years' practical experience, whereby the author has been enabled to divest the subject of much that has been considered mysterious and difficult to overcome, and render it more sure, profitable and interesting to every one than it has heretofore been. By E. W. Phelps.

Every Lady her own Flower Gardener;

Addressed to the Industrious and Economical only; containing Simple and Practical Directions for Cultivating Plants and Flowers; also, Hints for the Management of Flowers in Rooms, with brief Botanical Descriptions of Plants and Flowers. The whole in plain and simple language. By Louisa Johnson.

The Cow; Dairy Husbandry and Cattle Breeding.

By M. M. Milburn, and revised by H. D. Richardson and Ambrose Stevens. With Illustrations.

Wilson on the Culture of Flax;

Its Treatment, Agricultural and Technical: delivered before the New York State Agricultural Society, at the Annual Fair, held at Saratoga, in September last, by John Wilson, late President of the Royal Agricultural College at Cirencester, England.

Weeks on Bees.—A Manual;

Or, an Easy Method of Managing Bees in the most profitable manner to their owner; with infallible rules to prevent their destruction by the Moth; with an appendix by Wooster A. Flanders. Price 50 cts.

Pardee on Strawberry Culture.

A Complete Manual for the Cultivation of the Strawberry; with a description of the best varieties.

Also, notices of the Raspberry, Blackberry, Currant, Gooseberry, and Grape; with directions for their cultivation, and the selection of the best varieties. "Every process here recommended has been proved, the plans of others tried, and the result is here given." With a valuable appendix, containing the observations and experience of some of the most successful cultivators of these fruits in our country. Price 50 cts.

Elliott's American Fruit-Grower's Guide in Orchard and

Garden; Being a Compend of the History, Modes of Propagation, Culture, &c., of Fruit, Trees, and Shrubs, with descriptions of nearly all the varieties of Fruits cultivated in this country; and notes of their adaptation to localities, soils, and a complete list of Fruits worthy of cultivation. By F. R. Elliott, Pomologist. Price $1 25.

History of Wool, Cotton, Linen, Silk,

And other Fibrous Substances; including Observations on Spinning, Dyeing, and Weaving. Also, an Account of the Pastoral Life of the Ancients, their Social State, and attainments in the Domestic Arts. With Appendices on Pliny's Natural History; on the Origin and Manufacture of Linen and Cotton Paper; on Felting, Wetting, &c., deduced from copious and authentic sources. Illustrated by steel engravings. Price $2 50.

Buist's American Flower-Garden Directory;

Containing Practical Directions for the Culture of Plants, in the Flower-Garden, Hot-House, Green-House, Rooms or Parlor Windows, for every Month in the Year; with a Description of the Plants most desirable in each, the Nature of the Soil and Situation best adapted to their Growth, the Proper Season for Transplanting, &c.: with Instructions for erecting a Hot-House, Green-House, and Laying out a Flower-Garden; the whole adapted to either large or small Gardens: with instructions for preparing the Soil, Propagating, Planting, Pruning, Training, and Fruiting the Grape Vine. Price $1 25.

Pedder's Farmer's Land Measurer;

Or Pocket Companion; showing at one view, the Content of any Piece of Land, from Dimensions taken in Yards. With a set of Useful Agricultural Tables. Price 50 cts.

Chemical Field Lectures for Agriculturists;

Or, Chemistry without a Master. By Dr. Julius Adolphus Stockhardt, Professor in the Royal Academy of Agriculture at Tharand. Translated from the German. Edited, with notes, by James E. Teschemacher. Price $1 00.

Saxton's Rural Hand Books, ... $1 25

First Series containing Treatises on—

The Horse,	The Pests of the Farm,
The Hog,	Domestic Fowls, and
The Honey Bee,	The Cow.

Saxton's Rural Hand Books, ... $1 25

Second Series, containing—

Every Lady Her Own Flower Gardener,	Essay on Manures,
Elements of Agriculture,	American Kitchen Gardener,
Bird Fancier,	American Rose Culturist.

Saxton's Rural Hand Books. Third series, in preparation.

Thaër's Agriculture.

The Principles of Agriculture, by Albert D. Thaer; translated by William Shaw and Cuthbert W. Johnson, Esq., F. R. S. With a Memoir of the Author. 1 vol. 8vo. strong cloth. Price $2 00.

This work is regarded by those who are competent to judge, as one of the most beautiful works that has ever appeared on the subject of agriculture. At the same time that it is eminently practical, it is philosophical, and, even to the general reader, remarkably entertaining.

Von Thaer was educated for a physician; and, after reaching the summit of his profession, he retired into the country, where his garden soon became the admiration of the citizens; and when he began to lay out plantations and orchards, to cultivate herbage and vegetables, the whole country was astonished at his science in the art of cultivation. He soon entered upon a large farm, and opened a school for the study of Agriculture, where his fame became known from one end of Europe to the other.

This great work of Von Thaer's has passed through four editions in the United States, but it is still comparatively unknown. The attention of owners of landed estates in cities and towns, as well as those persons engaged in the practical pursuits of agriculture, is earnestly requested to this volume.

Guénon on Milch Cows:

A Treatise on Milch Cows, whereby the Quality and Quantity of Milk which any Cow will give may be accurately determined by observing Natural Marks or External Indications alone; the length of time she will continue to give Milk, &c., &c. By M. Francis Guénon, of Libourne, France. Translated by Nicholas P. Trist, Esq.; with Introductory Remarks and Observations on the Cow and the Dairy, by John S. Skinner. Illustrated with numerous Engravings. Price for single copies, neatly done up in paper covers, 37 1-2 cents; bound in cloth, 62 1-2 cents.

Dana's Muck Manual for the use of Farmers.

One of the most valuable works yet published. Price $1 00.

Chorlton's Cold Grapery.

50 cents.

The Fruit, Flower & Kitchen

Garden. By Patrick Neill, LL D , F. R S, adapted to the United States $1 25.

Ladies' Compan. to the Flower

Garden. By Mrs Loudon Edited by A. J. Downing. $1 25.

The Fruits and Fruit Trees

of America By A J Downing $1 50 , colored, $15

Dictionary of Modern Garden-

ing By Geo W Johnston Edited by David Landreth $1.50.

The Rose Fancier's Manual.

By Mrs Gore $1 50

Parsons on the Rose.

The Rose : its History, Poetry, Culture and Classification By S. B Parsons $1 50.

Hovey's Fruits of America ;

Containing richly-colored Figures and full Descriptions of all the Choicest Varieties cultivated in the United States $13

Rural Economy,

In its relations with Chemistry, Physics and Meteorology. By J B Boussingault Translated, &c, by George Law $1.

Liebig's Agricul. Chemistry.

Edited by Lyon Playfair, Ph D , F. G S , and William Gregory, M D , F R S E $1.

The Modern System of Far-

riery, as Practised at the Present Time at the Royal Veterinary College, and from Twenty Years' Practice of the Author, George Skevington, M. R V. C $5

The Horse's Foot,

And How to Keep it Sound By Wm. Miles 25 cts

Ewbank's Hydraulics:

A Descriptive and Historical Account of Hydraulic and other Machines for Raising Water. $2 50

The Fruit Garden.

By P Barry $1.25.

The Amern. Fruit Culturist ;

Containing Directions for the Culture of Fruit Trees in the Nursery, Orchard and Garden By John J. Thomas $1.

The Rose Manual.

By Robert Buist. 75 cts.

The Plants of Boston and

Vicinity. By Jacob Bigelow, M D $1.50.

Blake's Farmer's Every Day

Book. $2 50.

Catechism of Agr. Chemistry

and Geology. By J. F. W. Johnston 25 cts.

The Trees of America.

By D J Brown. $4.50

American Flower Garden

Directory By Robert Buist. $1.25

Loudon's Encyclopedia of Ar-

chitecture. $10

Loudon's Arboretum.

Eight Vols. $25.

Loudon on Gardening.

Loudon's Encyclopedia of Gardening $10.

Loudon on Agriculture.

Loudon's Encyclopedia of Agriculture $10.

Loudon on Trees, &c.

Loudon's Encyclopedia of Trees Shrubs, &c. $10

Loudon on Plants, &c.

Loudon's Encyclopedia of Plants, &c

The Farmer's Library.
Two vols. 8vo. English. $5.

The Farmer's Dictionary.
By D. P. Gardner. $1.75.

Practical Treatise on the Grape
Vine. By J. Fisk Allen. $1.

Agricultural Chemistry.
By Justus Liebig. Cloth, $1; cheap edition, 25 cents.

Animal Chemistry.
By J. Liebig. Cloth, 50 cents, cheap edition, paper, 25 cts.

Liebig's Complete Works,
In one vol. 8vo. $1.50.

American Cotton Spinner.
$1.

Cottage and Farm Houses.
By A. J. Downing. $2.

Country Houses.
By A. J. Downing. $4

Sportsman's Library.
By T. B. Johnson. English edition. $5.

Landscape Gardening.
By A. J. Downing. $3.50.

Cottage Residences.
By A. J. Downing. $2.

Chaptal's Agricul. Chemistry,
With Notes. $1.

American Husbandry.
By Gaylord and Tucker. $1.

Gardener's Dictionary.
By Geo. Don, F. L. S. 4 vols. quarto. $12

Journal of Agriculture.
Edited by John S. Skinner, 3 vols $6.

Downing's Horticulturist.
Half morocco. Per Vol. Yearly Vols. $3.75 half-yearly Vols, $2.

The Complete Produce Reck-
oner; showing the Value by Pound or Bushel. By R. Robbins. 75 cts.

The American Shepherd.
By L. A. Morrill. $1.

The Principles of Agriculture.
By Albert D. Thaer. $2.50.

Lectures to Farmers on Agri-
cultural Chemistry. By Alexander Petzholdts. 75 cts.

The Complete Farrier.
By John C. Knowlson. 25 cts.

The Complete Cow Doctor.
By J. C. Knowlson. 25 cts.

Milch Cows.
By Guenon. 38 cts.

A Home for All,
Or, a New, Cheap and Superior Mod of Building. By O. S. Fowler. 75 cts

The Gardener's Calendar.
By M. McMahon. $3.

The Poultry Breeder.
By George P. Burnham. 25 cts.

The American Fowl Breeder
25 cts.

The Farmer's Companion.
By Judge Buel 75 cts.

The Farmer's Instructor.
By Judge Buel. $1.

European Agriculture;
From Personal Observation. By Henry Coleman. 2 vols. $5. In one vol. $4.50.

The Gardener and Florist.
25 cts.

The Honey Bee.
By Bevan. 31 cts.

Elements of Pract. Agriculture.
By John F. N. ton. 50 cts.

Rogers' Scientific Agriculture.
75 cts.

Mills' Sportsman's Library.
$1.

Stable Talk and Table Talk.
$1.

Hawker & Porter on Shooting.
$2 75

Field Sports.
By Frank Forrester. 2 vols. $4.

Fish and Fishing.
By Frank Forrester. $2 50.

The American Angler's Guide.
By J J. Brown. $1 50

Johnson's Farmer's Encyclo-
pedia Edited by G Emerson. M D
$4

Scientific and Practical Agri-
culture. By Alonzo Gray. 75 cts

Armstrong on Agriculture.
50 cts

Wilson's Rural Encyclopedia.
4 vols. Illustrated. $18

Longstrath on the Honey Bee.
$1.25

Smith's Universal Hand Book.
$2 50.

Hovey's Magazine of Horticul-
ture Published monthly Per annum,
$2.

Barry's Horticulturist.
Published monthly. Per annum, $2

Gilpin's Landscape Garden-
ing English edition $2 50

Book of Flowers;
In which are described the various
Hardy Herbaceous Perennials, Annu-
als, Shrubby Plants and Evergreen
Trees desirable for Ornamental Pur-
poses By Jos Breck. 75 cts

Agriculture for Schools.
By Rev. J. L. Blake, D D $1

Text Book of Agriculture.
By Davis 50 cts

Cottages and Cottage Life.
By Elliott $2 25

Applied Chemistry.
By A Parnell. $1

The Vegetable Kingdom;
Or Handbook of Plants By L. D
Chapin. $1 25.

The Muck Manual.
A new edition. By Samuel L. Dana
$1

Youatt on the Horse.
Edited by J. S. Skinner. $1 50

Clater's Farrier.
50 cents

The American Herd Book.
By Lewis F. Allen. $3.

Browne's Trees of America.
Vol 1, 8vo. $4 50

Downing's Rural Essays.
$3.

American Flower Garden Di-
rectory By Robert Buist. $1.25.

The American Flora.
4 vols., colored plates $20.

Miner's   Domestic   Poultry
Book. Paper, 50 cts. ; cloth, 75 cts.

Stockhardt's Chemical Field
Lectures. $1.

Christy's Chemistry of Agri-
culture. 50 cts

Buchannan on Grape Culture
and Longworth on Strawberry 50 cts